Become the One

Heal Your Love Wounds & Find Your Inner Soulmate

By
EJ LOVE

First published in 2020 by EJ Love

© EJ Love
The moral rights of the author have been asserted.
This book is a SpiritCast Network Book

National Library of Australia Cataloguing-in-Publication data:

Author:	
	Emmajane, Love
Title:	
	Become The One; Heal Your Love Wounds and Find Your Inner Soulmate.
ISBN:	
	978-1-72175-363-5
Subjects:	
	Relationships, Sexuality, Personal Growth.

All rights reserved. Except as permitted under the Australian Copyright Act 1968 (for example, a fair dealing for the purposes of study, research, criticism or review), no part of this book may be reproduced, stored in a retrieval system, communicated or transmitted in any form or by any means without prior written permission. All enquiries should be made to EJ Love.

Editor-in-chief: Anita Saunders
Cover Design: Aldren The Lonestar

Disclaimer:
The material in this publication is of the nature of general comment only, and does not represent professional advice. It is not intended to provide specific guidance for particular circumstances and it should not be relied on as the basis for any decision to take action or not take action on any matter which it covers. Readers should obtain professional advice where appropriate, before making any such decision. To the maximum extent permitted by law, the author and publisher disclaim all responsibility and liability to any person, arising directly or indirectly from any person taking or not taking action based on the information in this publication.

This book is dedicated to every woman, man, and child who has experienced abuse.

May this book give you a voice when it hasn't felt safe for you to speak.

Hello, Amazing Being!

Thank you for taking this huge step to heal your love wounds, reclaim your power in your relationships, and come home to your inner soulmate.

I'm so excited to be sharing this so vulnerably with you and for it to be a profound and life-changing experience for you, as it has been for me!

Peer Support—Join the Facebook Tribe

Having support from others on the same healing journey in a safe community will keep you accountable and encourage you to keep going when the going gets tough. If you find yourself in resistance or procrastination this is usually right before you get to the real gold!

If you are on Facebook I encourage you to **add yourself to the Facebook Group. It can be found at** www.facebook.com/groups/ejlovetribe.

My team will approve your request to join shortly. This is a closed group so only those in the group can see the posts. It is a space of non-judgement where you can share your experiences as you read the book, ask questions, and get further support from myself and others.

Once you have been approved to join the group I encourage you to **introduce yourself and to share why you are choosing to read this book and what you would love to get out of it.** You only have to share what you feel comfortable with and you will also find others' vulnerable sharing will make you feel safe and supported.

Make a Commitment to Show Up for Yourself

Make sure you set aside some time each day or week to read and do the practices. I know we can get busy with life, but this book is what will help you have the life, love, and relationships you have always wanted.

If you get behind, don't stress or give up, I know you have got this! If you need support and accountability you can reach out to the Facebook group or to me and my team via email or social media (all these details are in the back of this book).

Now let's get ready to go on the deepest relationship healing journey of your life!

With all my love,

EJ xx

Table of Contents

Introduction 1

Chapter 1   Dear Ego, Get Out of My Way
So I Can Choose Love...17

Chapter 2   The Woundmate Experience..27

Chapter 3   Maturing the Masculine to Hold the Healthy
Feminine..65

Chapter 4   Embracing the Victimised Perspective 79

Chapter 5   Consciously Losing Your Shit...................................91

Chapter 6   Emotional Triggers as a Pathway to Self-Love 105

Chapter 7   The "Twin Flame" Spiritual Awakening 127

Chapter 8   Are You Ready for The One? 141

Chapter 9   Twin Flames and Narcissism 149

Chapter 10   Soulmate or Woundmate? 159

Chapter 11   The Re-Wounding...167

Chapter 12   The Rescuer and the Victim 175

Chapter 13   Narcissists, Empaths, and Co-Dependents 189

Chapter 14   Emotional Unavailability and Ghosting 205

Chapter 15	The Self-Sabotager and Friendzoner	215
Chapter 16	The Non-Committed Push-Puller	219
Chapter 17	The Avoidant Settler	225
Chapter 18	Reclaim Your Power in Love	233
Chapter 19	Coming Home to Your Inner Soulmate	249
Chapter 20	Self-Marriage Ceremony	263

Conclusion 279

Meet EJ Love 281

Recommended Resources 287

Testimonials 291

Acknowledgements..299

Introduction

"The love you seek is not outside of you, it is held within every fibre of your soul."

This book was originally written for every woman who has ever felt hurt by men and given her power away in romantic relationships.

However, I also wanted to make the healing journey in this book available for men and for those who are non-binary gender.

I feel it is so needed for men to be able to heal their relationship with themselves and the feminine. I have seen that they too have such a longing for love and to truly open their hearts. So even though the next few pages are written with women in mind, others will find that they resonate to experiencing this in their relationships too. You could also look at it in the sense of getting knowledgeable on the things women in your life might be going through or read the book from the perspective of your feminine and it will help you in this way.

This book is also very applicable for all sexual orientations and relationship styles, simply tailor the language and practices to suit your preference. All these practices are applicable to everyone, and can be used for all types of relationships too, not just romantic ones.

So please keep reading because there is some gold and deep healing for everyone throughout this book!

You Have Been Conditioned to Believe That Love Is Outside of Yourself

If you are anything like me, you have been conditioned since childhood to believe that true love comes via a romantic partner. Through fairy tales and romantic movies we have been sold woundmates, cleverly disguised as soulmates!

Because what really happens after "happily ever after"? … No one ever knows because that part of the story isn't told.

As a child you were most likely not taught how to relate in healthy ways, you were not taught how to fully feel all of your emotions, you were not told that people have wounds, traumas, and triggers that they are probably going to project onto you and you onto them! You were not shown how to manage any of that!

You were not taught how to consciously communicate or how to ask for what you need or how to have healthy boundaries. You were not shown that the most loving thing you can do is to actually speak your truth and put yourself first.

In fact, you were probably conditioned that it's selfish to ask for what you want and that you need to put others before yourself. You may have been shut down for speaking up and shown that speaking your truth could get you into trouble and you were probably shamed if you told a lie.

Throughout school you were taught there was right and wrong and that if you didn't get things right then there was something wrong with you. It was like no matter what you did you were never going to be good enough!

You were most likely shown that love was conditional. That to get someone's love you needed to behave a certain way and if you didn't show up that way, then you were not worthy of their love.

Introduction

You Then Started to Seek Love and Approval

As this cemented in your innocent brain over time, you sought this love and approval from others. This would often be wrapped up in an "ideal man" or "perfect woman." If you found them you would then put them before you and in that process you completely devalued yourself.

You may have moulded and changed who you were to make them happy and completely lost yourself all because you were so afraid to be abandoned or deemed to be unlovable.

And people do this time after time after time in all different relationships and areas of their lives and then they wonder—*Why am I not happy? Why don't I feel loved? I thought that once I found someone to love me then I would be happy.*

But this is because the person who you needed to love you was YOU all along!

You May Have Found Yourself Looking for "The One"

But as you were probably conditioned to believe, you thought that when you met your soulmate you would finally feel complete.

What you didn't know was that part of believing that the feeling of completeness was outside of yourself would in fact lead to you attracting unhealthy, co-dependent, and even narcissistic relationships.

You may have lost yourself so many times that you don't even know what it's like not to lose yourself in a relationship.

You may have often been left feeling so devastated and confused. You may have wondered why it is that you have attracted the wrong type of person, questioning if a healthy, loving relationship is even possible for you?

You may have been with people who didn't have the capacity to truly love and honour you and see you for the amazing being that deep down you know you are. You may have attracted people who have hurt you, abused you, ignored you, rejected you, abandoned you, cheated on you, disrespected you, betrayed you, manipulated you, and lied to you.

You Have Given So Much of Yourself

All the while you have given so much of yourself, you have supported them, loved them, cared for them, and even sacrificed your own wants trying to give them everything you thought that they wanted. And still it wasn't enough to make them happy; instead, you just ended up feeling used and even betrayed.

Perhaps you unknowingly or knowingly became a little bit bitter towards men and have stopped being able to see that there are really decent, kind, healthy men out there. Men that actually want to give to you, support you, honour you, and love you just the way you are.

Yes, they do exist!

Maybe you do meet these healthy men and somehow you are just not into the "decent ones," the ones that actually would love to treat you like a Queen. You may have ended up sabotaging your connection with them or they always seem to be taken already!

And what about the men who seem oh so lovely at first? Let's not forget them! They say all the right things. They seem too good to be true, and then one day, they suddenly change on you.

They disappear or they hurt you in an unthinkable way and it's like everything they ever said at the beginning was one giant lie. You feel like a real sucker, especially when their actions never seem to line up with their words. So how can you trust anything a man says ever again?

Introduction

You Wonder Why You Deserve to Be Treated Like This

You can never quite understand why this happens to you!

You are a good, kind, decent person that just gives and gives and you can't imagine what you have done to deserve any of this treatment!

You wore your heart on your sleeve and because you never healed properly from an earlier wound in your life, you have kept replaying out this same hurt.

Here you are now, having been burnt far too many times in your relationships. You may have at one point decided to give up on love altogether, thinking that it is just easier to be alone. You closed your heart and you told yourself that "I won't let anyone ever hurt me again."

The problem with that is that you closed your heart not just to another, but to your own love. You shut yourself down from feeling all the emotional pain, it was just all too much.

So you were done with looking for love for a while. You were just going to keep yourself so busy, focus on your career, be strong and independent, and make life on your own amazing.

Then one day, when 'the time was right', you thought your soulmate would just come along!

You Felt Empty and Alone at Times

But yet, no matter how much you focused on keeping yourself busy, there was still something missing inside of you. You may have felt an emptiness at night time just before you went to bed, perhaps doubting yourself and questioning the choices you have made.

And this is when you felt that incompleteness that sits inside your soul.

You then question—what am I doing all of this for?

Because all that "busyness" has simply been an avoidance tactic, to avoid feeling the pain of the emptiness and not feeling truly loved.

You have been trying to fill that void with all this stuff and then hopefully it would be filled by someone else when you were finally "ready" to meet the one!

But whilst your fears and emotional pain still sits inside of you, there is never going to be a time when you will be ready.

This may be the very reason why you are here, because you want to be ready to become "the one" for that special someone.

But the feeling of incompleteness has nothing to do with anyone else, it's because you haven't fully felt the depth of your own love first. That piece of your heart that feels missing is there inside of you.

It's only that you have it so heavily guarded that it simply cannot be felt and now here you are ready to break through those chains and fall in love - with yourself.

This Book Isn't About Becoming "The One" for Someone Else

It's about becoming "the one" inside of you first.

It's about helping your soul to recognise and feel that you are already whole.

You are not half of a soul that needs to be with their soulmate to feel complete, you are already a whole soul who chooses who they are in a relationship with from a place of wholeness rather than lack.

Then you won't unconsciously choose someone because they fill a void and meet your need for love and approval, you consciously choose that person because they simply enhance your already fulfilled feeling of love and happiness inside of you.

Introduction

This is where healthy relationships begin. It begins with you having a healthy, deeply loving relationship with yourself. Because the people who show up in your life will always show up as your reflection and I'm guessing that you would want to be with someone who also has a healthy relationship with themselves too.

Would you want to be with someone who is with you because you fill their voids?

No, that doesn't sound nice when I put it that way, does it?!

So although this book isn't designed to call in your soulmate, I can guarantee that if you do all the work that I set out for you right through until the end, then you are going to naturally attract people who hold soulmate energy, because your energy will now align with theirs. I call this "Soulmate Alignment".

If you are already in a relationship you will be able to evolve it into a happier, healthier one or have the strength to leave one that is toxic.

You Will Become Your Own Soulmate First

Since like attracts like, when you become your own soulmate first, you will attract others who are also on the same journey of self-love and wholeness. This will be in all areas of your life too, not just romantic relationships.

What this book is designed for is to heal the wounds of your past relationships, to dive deep into the unconscious patterns that have kept you attracting unhealthy relationships, to bring down the walls of protection over your heart, and to open you to feeling the love that you are.

This is where you will then feel worthy and safe to receive the love from someone who has the genuine capacity to love YOU, not love you because you feel their voids.

This book is really about being your own soulmate first. It is about letting go of the need to have someone else to love and approve of you that has led to co-dependent relating.

It is about being in the relationship with yourself that you always wanted with someone else.

It is learning how to give yourself the love that you always longed for and to feel it on a level that you have never felt before.

Healing Your Relationship with Men

This book is NOT about making men wrong or telling you that you don't need a man.

It is about being able to heal the wounds you have experienced with men in the past, so that you can see them from a more loving perspective.

It is about being able to see them through the eyes of love which will have them then reflect this back to you.

It is also about seeing how men have been the reflection of your inner masculine and learning how to love and mature this part of yourself.

It is about evolving your own inner masculine energy to hold you and keep you safe, rather than expecting man to do that for you, whilst still remaining open to receiving it from them.

It's about helping you feel safe to be in your true feminine power. A power that is vulnerable and receptive and feels safe to let go of control and surrender.

Part of this means looking for and owning the ways that you too have hurt men.

This is how you start to reclaim your feminine power.

A power that comes from an open heart, not from a place of protection.

Introduction

And what happens when you learn and access all of this?

You Will Be in Relationships From an Empowered Place

You will still enjoy being loved by others, but you won't rely on someone else to love and approve of you, because you already love and approve of yourself.

So when you are not being treated lovingly by someone, you will have the courage to make a stand for yourself and set healthy boundaries. That may mean walking away sometimes, but you will do it with your head held high and your heart still open.

You will do this not from a place of over-protection or asserting unhealthy masculine energy, you will do this from a place of honouring your boundaries and speaking from your heart and authentic vulnerability. This comes from your inner masculine and feminine working in union together.

You will finally have the willingness to walk away from anything that does not serve you!

If You Are Currently in a Relationship

Now let me also speak to the person reading this who is currently in a romantic relationship.

There is a reason you felt drawn to this book and I'm imagining that it is because either you feel unhappy or unfulfilled within yourself or a relationship and you want to either turn that around or feel confident enough to set some boundaries, or leave the relationship if it's not healthy.

If your relationship with your partner is healthy, this book will give you plenty of practices to help you to have a much more conscious relationship and you can use these tools together, or even better, both read the book!

If both people in a relationship healed their past relationships and wounds it sure would prevent a lot of unnecessary triggering and projecting!

If You are Not a Woman

I want to acknowledge you for reading this far! You may be thinking that this book isn't designed for you or perhaps you are curious to go on this healing journey yourself or to even understand more about how women think. The beauty of what I teach in this book is that it can be applied to anyone.

When I use the terms masculine and feminine, I don't mean man or woman. Everyone holds both of these energies within them and by reading this book you will evolve yourself as you integrate these energies in you into a healthier place.

Men have had their feminine energy suppressed even more than women and therefore it is important for them to reclaim their own feminine power and evolve their inner masculine into a healthy place where they can be grounded and present enough inside themselves so they feel safe to feel their emotions and be vulnerable. This then reflects out to the relationships they have with women and the kind of women they attract.

So you will be able to heal your past relationships by following my healing journey and doing the practices in this book. The added bonus is that you are actually going to learn A LOT about women and how we often think and feel towards men.

You may even want to gift this book to all the women in your life who you think really could do with some healing around men! I'll be going more into how women unconsciously hurt men in chapters 3 and 12 – yes, you can thank me later for that!

By healing our past resentments and then understanding each other and celebrating our differences, I believe this is truly possible.

Introduction

One of my greatest passions is to end the separation between the genders.

So even though this book was originally written for women, it too applies to you and I really hope you do read it, because it will change your life and your relationships and hopefully help you to understand women in a way that helps you to relate more authentically with them and with your inner feminine.

Would You Want to Marry Yourself?

Think about that question. Would you really want to marry you? And if the answer is no, then I would be asking.. why is that? Because that is what this book is going to help you with! I want you to be at a place by the end of this journey where you feel you love yourself enough to marry yourself!

In the final stages of this book you will be given an opportunity to do you very own self-marriage ceremony.

Now perhaps self-marriage isn't for you, and you don't have to do anything that doesn't feel aligned. Instead you can see the final chapter as simply a self-love ceremony - a way to celebrate and complete the journey you have just been on.

This book is really for anyone who wants to deepen their level of self-love and have a soul-connected relationship with themselves! To be someone you would want to marry, because you have to live with yourself for the rest of your life!

Throughout the book I am going to give you practical tools to apply immediately that will help you to show up differently in both your relationship with yourself and in relationships with others.

I will then give you the step-by-step process to hold your very own Self-Marriage Ceremony or Self-Love Commitment Ceremony. This is to integrate and honour the deep healing journey I will have taken you through and to commit to showing up inside your new empowered truth.

You need to, however, read the whole book and do the practices before you can do this part, because the ceremony is put together from self-discoveries that you will have made during the previous chapters.

You Will Be a Much Happier, and More Loved-Up Version of Yourself

I can guarantee you that once you finish this book you will never look at yourself, men, women, and relationships in the same way ever again and you will understand why everything in your relationships has happened to you and have created a whole new possibility for your future.

You will feel more whole. You will feel more connected to who you are at the soul level. You will see the world with fresh eyes and a more open heart. You will have evolved and become more integrated in both your masculine and feminine energies. You will have deepened into a whole new level of self-love.

I believe that reading this book will be one of those things that you wish you did years ago, because you know it would have saved you a hell of a lot of heartache!

Make the Time and the Commitment to Do the Work

I spent 18 months intensively healing myself after my last abusive relationship. I have condensed everything I did in that time into this book because I really don't want it to take you 18 months!

If you really commit to doing the practices I set for you in this book, you can do it in as little as a few weeks. However, I have designed this book in a way where you can use the tools and practices over and over again when new issues and triggers come up in your relationships. I've made it like a healing 'go to' bible.

Introduction

A few weeks to heal a lifetime of heartache and to prevent you from experiencing it again: I promise you, it is more than worth it.

As I mentioned before this is not just another self-help book to "find the one." It is a real, raw, and vulnerable account of my journey to heal myself from the hurt and abuse I personally experienced with men.

I know that everyone can relate to my story in one way or another. Most of my clients come from my social media blogs and videos, where I vulnerably share my experiences and stories.

So many people reach out to me and say "It's like you were telling my story, it's like you were talking directly to me."

My hope is that you too will resonate to my story and find big pieces of gold and plenty of "ahas" throughout it.

My Biggest Mission With This Book Is to End Abuse

When I tell my story, I know that I am telling so many other people's stories too. I know that I am a voice for so many women, many who don't feel safe enough to share their experiences. Some of these women are still in abusive and unhealthy relationships and my hope is that one day this book will end up in every one of those women's hands, as well as in the hands of men who have also experienced abuse.

When someone heals themselves from past abuse, not only do they prevent it from happening again, but they also heal it for future generations and for the collective consciousness. If this book was read by everyone who had ever been abused, I believe that in generations to come we could end abuse on a global scale.

If you know anyone who has been abused and needs help healing from their past relationships, please do them one of the greatest favours by recommending this book to them, or giving it as a gift.

Let the Journey Back to Love Begin!

You are about to re-condition yourself because you are here to un-learn that love is conditional and remember your truth—that you are love.

That YOU, my fellow beautiful human being, are unconditional love!

That the love you seek is not outside of you, that it is held within every fibre of your soul.

This is the part where you heal your wounds that have stopped you from feeling all the love that you already are.

This is the place where you learn how to use your emotional triggers as a pathway to your healing that will deepen you into greater self-love.

This is the time where you take your power back from all the times that you have given it away trying to get love from others.

This is where you start to change the stories that have been running around in your head over and over that have told you that you will never do or be enough to deserve love.

Because how can that even be possible?

How can it be possible that you cannot deserve love, when you, beautiful soul, you are love?

Love isn't something that you get, find, or deserve, love is something that YOU ARE.

So it is my duty and honour to take you on this journey, a journey into your heart to find your path back to love.

Your life may have taken you away from that path, but as you turn each page of this book you take one small step back onto that path, until

Introduction

one day you find yourself back to where it all began—in your own innocent, loving heart.

And from that place of innocence anything becomes possible!

So if you are up for that, then you are going to love this book!

Chapter 1

Dear Ego, Get Out of My Way So I Can Choose Love

"This is not going to be love and light. This is going to be shake-your-whole-fucking-world-up, shatter-your- heart-until-it-breaks-open shit."

It was November 2014 and by this stage in my life I thought I had it all down pat. I was a healer and coach who was teaching self-love. I had now awakened and transformed my life! The amount of spiritual work I had done on myself, the workshops, the healings, yoga, meditation, dancing, the list goes on ...

I thought I had my shit sorted. So now I could finally attract someone who would be at my *"vibration,"* someone that had the capacity to love me because I now loved myself. I was now truly ready and open for love, wasn't I?

Well ... I thought I was, but oh no ... no ... no...

My inner soulmate decided to enlighten me:

You think you have it all sorted, do you? Oh, that's very sweet. But you are now going to attract someone who's going to show you all your deepest wounds and sorry to tell, it's not gonna be pretty.

Actually I'm not sorry, you need this. It's going to challenge you like you could never in your worst nightmares have imagined.

You think you love yourself now; well, as I am your inner being, I have to tell you that there are parts of you that you don't think are lovable. They are so deeply buried that you can't even see them right now. I'm here to show you that they are lovable, but for you to really see and feel that I'm going to have to bring up the deepest wounds you have buried where you have created "unlovableness."

This is where HE comes in. This man you attract, he's going to reflect this by not only triggering these wounds, but attacking all these parts of you that you deep down feel are unlovable. Which of course are only the parts of himself he can't stand.

There will be manipulation, lies, and narcissistic abuse that preys on your martyr, rescuer and caretaking roles that you have highly developed and deeply engrained.

In the process you will completely lose yourself to try and make the relationship work. Because you think that this is finally your time for love. Be prepared to doubt and question yourself and your abilities constantly. Be prepared to be crushed to the core of your soul.

Don't worry though, I've got you.

You will rise up from this ... eventually. I promise.

It may take a little while because your wounds and trauma bonds are going to keep you stuck in this toxic dynamic.

But one day you'll get to a point where you feel like you are not really living anymore, like a weak shadow of your former self, and you'll reach out to me because you know in truth this man is not the one for you.

I did tell you that from the start, but no, no, you didn't listen to me. That's okay though, I'll forgive you and then we will make sure this never happens again!

You Will Heal Like You've Never Healed Before

So we'll devise a plan for you to leave for good and then you'll never look back.

That's when you'll be ready and willing to really listen to me ... finally!!!

I'm your deeper truth. I'm your unconscious consciousness. I'm the one who you've really been looking for all this time. I'm your inner being - I'm your true soulmate!

I will then show you how to heal like you have never healed before and then you will fucking rise up!

You will dig into the mud, the shit, and the shame. Oh, the shame!!

I hear ya. Fuck the shame! Let's not forget the guilt either.

But you have to learn to love the shame and the guilt. They are here to show you even more of your truth and then you'll learn that they aren't real either and then you'll thank them and let them go. It's only the meaning you make that makes them real for you. I'm going to show you all of that too.

Love is the only thing that's real, everything else you just made up!

Oh, yes, you did. You created all of it. You'll want to blame everyone else, especially him, but, honey, you unconsciously chose this and taking self-responsibility will empower you.

Remember the first time you got really hurt?

You didn't make that happen to you. But that's when you created the meaning behind it and that is where the hurt comes from, the meaning. It's not what happens to you, but what happens through you.

And what if I told you that life was actually happening FOR you?

But you have been living inside of this meaning and unconsciously choosing every relationship to prove that it's all true.

Yes, I hear you saying that you understand this already and you've been working on this shit for years! But you didn't go deep enough, you didn't quite get to the heart of the source wound, the first ever soul-crushing thing that happened to you, the ego-survival mechanism kicker inner, the one that's been protecting you all along.

You didn't fully meet your SHADOWS.

You've only learned to love the parts of yourself that you felt you could love. You learned to love the light in you and that, my dear, was only scratching the surface!

I Saw You Spiritually Bypassing Your "Twin Flame" Narcissist

I saw you praying to your Angels, meditating on your chakras, getting energy healings, cutting cords, and putting crystals in your bra so you could heal yourself from that "twin flame" connection that kept you in so much unnecessary confusion, longing, and torment.

Hoping that one day if you healed yourself enough he would want to be with you.

I saw how you were spiritually bypassing by your refusal to see the truth of his narcissistic behaviour. I know you wanted to be with him so damn badly that you completely blinded yourself to it all.

So when you finally accepted that you would never be with him it was time to bring in the next man who would bring all of this into the light for you to see.

A narcissist of a new kind, the more dangerous kind, the covert kind.

This is because you had not learned how to love the places where you feel the deepest shame. You haven't even been aware of what these really are for you. But don't worry, you will see it all, and I've got your back in this.

Dear Ego, Get Out of My Way So I Can Choose Love

I'm taking you to those depths, to shake you up so that you can finally see all the ways that you have been dishonouring yourself and shaming yourself, because that's exactly why these men dishonour and blame you.

They have been the reflection of your inner blame – your unowned shame and shadows.

The good news is, that once I take you to this depth, you can then choose differently!

You can completely destroy all the shit you made up and you can create a new empowered meaning and live and relate to people inside of that instead.

You've done some spiritual groundwork and I praise you for that, but no more of this fluffy unicorns, sparkly rainbows, and love and light shit. This is not going to be love and light.

This is going to be shake-your-whole-fucking-world-up, shatter-your-heart-until-it-breaks-open shit.

Yes, I'm here to tell you that your heart is going to break like it's never broken before. It's not breaking over him though. It's breaking open for yourself. This is something new for you, because this time you'll make the choice to heal your deepest, darkest wounds.

Damn scary, confusing, profound, and exciting all at the same time. I know it may not feel exciting at times.

But just trust me, I've got you.

You have been unconsciously choosing this

It's these damn wounds that are keeping people from CHOOSING from their heart. The meanings, the stories, the conditioning, the deep need to keep yourself so damn safe all the time.

Well it's fucking your love life up. It's all bullshit. It's not real!

Have you noticed when you try to keep yourself safe, that's usually when you get hurt the most? Guess what, you chose it! Then you decide you have to keep yourself even more protected. You turn away from love when it's right there in front of you—inside of you!

Instead, you give the ego more evidence as to why all your made-up stories are true.

"See, I told you no one wants me, I'm not lovable, I always get hurt, I can't trust people, men are liars and assholes, everybody leaves me, I get rejected, I always get cheated on."

But you CHOSE IT. ALL OF IT. But you weren't even aware of it because you chose it unconsciously.

So my question to you is - do you want to stay in your victimised story or do you want to become empowered and be able to make conscious choices?

Your Ego Has Been Winning the War Inside of You

You, in the past, like most people, have chosen to close your heart again and again, heartbreak after heartbreak. Since your very first heartbreak it's not your heart that has been choosing. It's your ego and it has been winning the war inside of you.

It has said "Oh no, I can't get hurt again, I'll shut the heart off so it doesn't even get to have a choice."

But deep down your heart is yearning to feel love.

This little voice inside says "Please let me love again, please, I want to choose love, please, please, let me choose this time."

The ego claims "No, I'm here to protect you, I'll choose someone you could never truly fall in love with, I'll let you feel like you can though.

Dear Ego, Get Out of My Way So I Can Choose Love

But really, I'm just keeping you safe and I'll choose someone who's not emotionally available to you or is all wrong for you.

I can't have you falling in love with someone amazing, that's way too risky. They will just reject you or leave you like the others. I think it's just easier to be alone. I'll prove it to you, it's better just you and me, you'll see. I'm not going to let you truly open up to anyone. It's just too scary for you to be vulnerable.

So I'll only allow you to share the parts of you I think people could love. I promise I'll never share the parts I think are completely unlovable, those parts I'll hide. If anyone does ever see them I'll make sure I get you out of there as fast as possible through some kind of self-sabotage."

So just when you think you chose from your heart. Sorry to tell you, but you chose from your ego again!

So what if you could just choose differently?

What if you could feel safe to choose from your heart?

Do you even know what choosing from your heart looks like?

If You Chose From Your Heart

If the heart had a bigger voice than the ego, it would reply:

"I know you are just here to protect me, but I don't choose to live from protection or safety. I choose to live from love. I am willing to be vulnerable and risk being hurt.

I choose love and I choose me, because I am love. So ego, get out of my way so I can choose love!"

Now hold your hand over your heart and tell it:

"No more feeling sorry for yourself, heart. No more keeping yourself small. I miss you. The world misses you. It is time to be all of you. It's time for you to be empowered and feel and know your worth. It is safe for you to be seen. I have got you in this. Let's rise together NOW"

Empower your heart to choose what it really, really wants and to know that it is safe and free to fully express itself.

You cannot choose love from your ego. The ego chooses from safety. You cannot choose love when your heart is not open to it. You will FEEL when your heart cracks open.

To open it you have to heal your deepest wounds. You have to find all the things you think are unlovable about you and love the shit out of them! Then you feel safe to be seen, then you feel safe to be truly loved by another.

Do you really want to keep repeating this same pattern over and over?

I didn't think so!

So it's decided then. You are choosing love. Even with all the buts, excuses, and maybes you can just choose now.

All right, good. Let's do this shit!

And once you are doing this deep work on yourself, you're going to share this with the world; oh yes, you are going to be vulnerable!

People need to know how to find their own truth in love and you are here to help them do that.

You are going to help them dig into and heal their deepest wounds and empower themselves to choose from their heart.

I know you probably wish I told you this earlier. I did tell you, but you couldn't hear me over the loud voice of protection in your head. I was only a whisper back then, but now that you are finally listening to me I am here to help you rise up from this.

Dear Ego, Get Out of My Way So I Can Choose Love

And this is when you will finally come home to who you truly are.

With loving presence,

Your Inner Soulmate xx

#LOVEPRACTICE: A LETTER FROM YOUR INNER SOULMATE

Set aside at least 30 mins for this journalling practice. You can also do it as a meditation and ask to receive messages from your deepest truth.

Journalling helps us to connect to our subconscious and to our inner being.

Begin by getting comfortable. Write at the top of the page 'Dear (your name)'. Then get clear on the area you want to receive messages on, close your eyes and simply ask your inner soulmate or deepest truth to come forward to speak you. You may receive sounds, words, visuals and begin writing these down or taking a mental note.

If you struggle to receive anything, just put pen to paper and start writing whatever comes out, even if it starts with 'I don't know what to write right now, but what I do know is…'.

Here are some extra prompts to guide you:-

'If I truly loved myself in this area I would… '

'I know the one thing that is really holding me back is…'

'I know what I really need to do is…'

Chapter 2
The Woundmate Experience

"The one that would bring me down into the depths of my core wounds and break me the fuck open so deeply to my own love"

So before I share with you the story of the relationship that would crush me to the core of my soul (yet at the same time completely break my heart open) I want you to know that this is NOT a poor-me story.

I don't want you to feel sorry for me. Even though I have experienced abuse, I do not see myself as a victim of it. This is a story about empowerment. This is a story about rising up after breaking down. This is a story that ended in making amends and a commitment to myself that I would never allow this to happen ever again.

And at the same time doing whatever I could to keep my heart open to love even after experiencing abuse. I am sharing this so that I empower other people to rise up when they feel like giving up. Inspiring them to keep their hearts open when they have been hurt so badly that they think the only safe way forward is to shut themselves off to love again.

However, I'm initially going to tell this story from more of a victimised perspective and as we move through the book you will see the story flip into an empowered one, which is exactly what I will be guiding you through with your own story.

After healing myself from abuse, I learned how to love men again and I have even run workshops for women on understanding and loving men.

You may have been so burnt by men that it may be difficult for you to imagine loving them right now, but by the end of this book, I imagine that will have changed! A big part of this begins with loving our own masculine energy which we will be doing throughout the book.

Hurt People Hurt People

I don't believe anyone is inherently bad and I like to identify that there is a difference between the being and the behaviour. I believe that we act in unconscious ways that are unloving to ourselves and to others from a place of pain, fear, and survival. Many people, particularly narcissists, have experienced so much trauma in their early life that they have blocked it out and they have a complete lack of empathy for others. It's not really their fault that they are like that, because on a soul level, they are still made up of love. It's just that their ego has created this false mask to protect themselves from their deep insecurities being seen; unfortunately it means they act in very manipulative and abusive ways that we have borne the brunt of. As the saying goes "hurt people hurt people."

Marshall Rosenberg, the author of *Non-Violent Communication,* says "Even the most horrific crimes are tragic attempts to get precious needs met." This is not to say that what these men did was acceptable and we are never, ever responsible for someone else's feelings, reactions, or actions. I am certainly not perfect myself and have made my fair share of unconscious choices that have hurt myself and others. But I have chosen to heal myself, self-reflect, own my parts in all of it, set healthy boundaries, and ultimately I have empowered myself and become more conscious of my choices so I can show up differently next time.

So bearing all that in mind, let's go back to where it all began …

Oh How I Loved Love and All of Its Potential

Firstly, my last name actually is Love! I really was born with it. I decided that meant that I was born for love and I must do everything I can to find it. I had been looking for it my whole life—outside of myself.

It didn't even occur to me that love actually was inside of me. It didn't occur to me that I could actually be an embodiment of love!

Ever since I can remember I was in love with love. My parents were the "perfect couple," openly affectionate towards one another; you could tell just how in love they were. The only time I ever saw them fight was over money.

There was a picture on the wall just outside my bedroom that said "How to know you are in love—you can't eat, you can't sleep, you can't stop thinking about the person …"

I remember those three lines so vividly. I read it almost every day. Unknowingly it was becoming engrained into my subconscious mind and I couldn't wait until the day I got to experience this "in love" feeling that people seemed to have when they met their soulmate - 'the one'!

I Was Hooked on the Idea of Meeting My Soulmate

Growing up watching fairy tales and witnessing my parents have a very close and loving relationship made me deeply desire that too. If there was one thing I wanted the most out of life, it was to be with my soulmate. So, at just 17 years old, when I thought I found my soulmate (*seems silly saying that now*), I got married. That's right, I got married at 17!

Justin and I married in secret at the local registry office. I had forged my mum's signature on the marriage licence, because there was no way she would ever have approved of this marriage! My now ex-husband was even banned from her house because of the poor way he treated me. They didn't even know that we were still dating; none of my family approved of him and so eventually I rebelled and moved out of home.

Before we got married the relationship had already been emotionally and mentally abusive. He would spend most of his time playing video games, gambling, or smoking weed. He would ignore me for days and then pay me attention when he wanted sex or needed money. That's when I associated my worth with money and sex. All I saw was this "bad boy" who seemed fun to hang out and have sex with, who made me feel good when he gave me attention. But unconsciously he was helping me avoid the pain of my parents' separation and the perceived loss of my Dad and our family unit.

He would be super loving one minute and then pushing me away, lying to me and telling me to piss off the next. I often felt invisible, unwanted, unloved, used, ignored, and rejected. But on the flipside of that, when he was being nice to me and paying me attention, I felt so incredibly loved and wanted. It was like one massive high-intensity emotional rollercoaster that I was so addicted to getting back on repeatedly!

We Would Break Up and Get Back Together So Many Times

When another woman came into the picture whenever we were broken up, I couldn't bear the thought of him being with someone else, so I would take him back.

I thought that if I married him that commitment meant that he did truly love me and that things would then change. I thought he would now stop ignoring me and put me first. But I couldn't have been more wrong. If anything, the abuse got worse. A year and a half into the marriage it started to get physical.

Eventually I knew it was over when when I lay there on the ground after he had smashed my head into a wall a few times.

It started when his friend had been calling me fat and ugly whilst at an internet cafe one day. Justin just sat there not defending me. I said "I'm your wife, aren't you going to say something?". He completely ignored me and in that moment all the resentment and anger of the past two years that had built up came out and I completely lost control and punched him in the nose.

I could not believe I could ever do something like that, who was this person I had become? I wasn't a violent person - this wasn't me! I ran out of the cafe crying, I felt awful, so I went back in and I immediately offered to take him to the doctor's. He ignored me and started walking out down the alley. I followed him and that was when he grabbed me by the neck, yelled into my face, hit my head into the wall and then threw me down on the ground. I remember lying there on the hard concrete watching him and his friend just walk away, they didn't even look back to see if I was okay. I blamed myself.

Later that same day his mum told my mum about our secret marriage. I'll never ever forget that look of disappointment on my mum's face, but now that she knew the full truth she was able to support me in finally leaving him for good.

We stopped contact immediately. I separated from him and moved from New Zealand to Australia four months later. By the end of the two years my self-esteem and self-worth were almost non-existent.

Reflecting on this experience I clearly saw how I gave my power away right from the very start of the relationship. I had actively pursued a man who was unhealthy and essentially unavailable. We will explore why this was more deeply later in the book.

It was now time for me to move on from him and start a new life.

Nothing Felt Better Than Being Sexy and Desirable

But by moving on, I meant I "numbed." Food was my comfort, but then purging it because I hated myself so much. I couldn't stand what I saw in the mirror anymore; how could anyone love me if I wasn't skinny and pretty? This is when my ten year battle with bulimia began.

I lost a heap of weight and suddenly was being noticed by men and having a lot of casual sex. I was going out clubbing, drinking, and being told how hot and sexy I was; it felt amazing. My self-esteem grew and I seemed to have this newfound confidence; it was like I was a whole new person.

A couple of years later I met a charismatic party boy, who also liked to gamble and take drugs. I too was partying a lot now and taking drugs most weekends.

After being friends for months, when we finally admitted we both liked each other and it then moved super fast! I moved into his house; he then left his job and I started supporting him. He soon started to act very paranoid and suspicious and every time he drank he would flip out and accuse me of things that made no sense and then get violent, mostly trying to hurt himself or break things.

When I tried to leave him, he threatened me and eventually the violence turned towards me and my property. I always felt sorry for him though. I could see that he had a good heart and was remorseful and I would then take him back.

This was the pattern. He would get violent, I would break up with him, and a few days later he would be apologising and we would get back together. This cycle went on for months. I knew it wasn't healthy, but I didn't know how to get out of it.

Plus his charming character meant he was always surrounded by women and because we lived in a smaller beachside town, when we were broken up I would see him out all the time with them. This would trigger the fuck out of me, and that's when I would usually take him back!

I knew that the only way for me to end this was if I left the town. So I packed up my bags and moved to Sydney to start a new life. He immediately started a relationship with someone else which felt incredibly heartbreaking for me, I wondered "how could he just move on so quickly?" Did I not mean anything to him?"

But I eventually 'moved on'… again.

This simply meant more numbing!

Why Was I Always Drawn to the "Wrong" Type of Man?

I told myself that I needed to be single for a while. I just wanted to have fun! I had now put up walls of protection around my heart and was numbing my pain with all this so-called "fun."

Although I met and had sex with plenty of men, there were only a few that I ever allowed myself to really fall for. Can you guess which ones they were? The users, the compulsive liars, the conmen, the cheaters, the abusers—yes, I had them all! It was like there was a sticker on my forehead that said "sucker" on it! Why were they always the ones I would get attached to the most and find the hardest to let go of?

Sometimes I would wonder why it was that other people found someone genuine to love them, but not me. Why did I always end up being attracted to the wrong type of man? What had I done to deserve being hurt like this?

I would repeatedly feel rejected and unwanted. I would then go into more numbing—more distractions, more "busyness," more sex, more partying, more purging, more smoking!

The truth was, I didn't feel worthy of love, except I didn't know that's what was going on back then. I was unconsciously sabotaging myself by not even making myself available to the men who I could actually have a healthy relationship with. The only way I would become available for this kind of love was to heal my heart from my past pain to feel my worthiness.

Swinging, Escorting and Getting Sexy on TV

Fast forward a few years and I had created a very sexy social life which included running my own swinger's parties. I was now heavily into the swinger's scene and through running these parties I ended up kind of just falling into the sex industry and becoming an escort (aka sex worker). This is when my alter ego, Claudia Jade L'Amore, was born! I would travel around Australia living in and out of hotels seeing escort clients and helping other women to become escorts.

I felt so much freedom living this travel lifestyle and doing whatever I wanted when I wanted! The money was like nothing I had ever made before and I couldn't believe I had been having sex for free for so long!

I actually have many interesting stories about my time as a swinger and how I got into the sex industry and my experiences in it, those stories are for a future book and some can also be found on my blog.

Most of the money I made from escorting went into starting a charity for a disabled client, running sexy themed events and setting up my own online TV channel called SexyON TV where I interviewed porn stars and sex educators. To the outside world it appeared as though I lived a dream life hanging out with adult stars, touring the country, and going to VIP parties.

But I was only feeling happiness in moments when I was "busy" with all this "stuff" which mainly came from experiences outside of myself. Underneath all these feel-good fixes I was not truly happy. I was just busy trying to fill my life up to avoid feeling the emptiness, just like I had been doing for the last ten years of my life!

I then received an opportunity to be interviewed by a porn company to see if I wanted to take the next step and move into making porn. I attended the interview, but I needed to take some to think about it. I knew this was a very big, life-changing decision.

My ego was pulling me one way and my soul was really telling me it wasn't part of my journey.

A part of me found the idea of becoming a porn star exciting and thrilling, but the other part of me felt very apprehensive.

But I wouldn't have to make that decision yet - because that's when he came into my world.

My "twin flame".

The Sliding Doors Moment

I met the man I thought was my twin flame; let's call him Charlie. I'm not going to tell you this story yet, I'm going to save that for later chapters in the book when we dive into understanding twin flames, soulmates, and woundmates. It's a juicy story and will be worth holding out for!

After I met him I started to question everything I was doing in my life and I decided that making porn was not really for me at all, I even considered giving up escorting to be with him.

Fast forward to three weeks after our first meeting, I was now left feeling highly confused and devastated by him running away from the intensity of our connection. Instead of making porn here I was in Bali on a retreat doing yoga, meditation, and learning all about my chakras. Three weeks before this I didn't even know what the hell a chakra was!

This was the beginning of my spiritual awakening. Instead of porn, I would do spirituality!

In this sliding doors moment in my life, I had finally chosen to look inside of myself as I started to feel all of the emotions that I had kept buried since the heartbreak of my ex-husband and childhood. Over the next 18 months I spent a lot of my time and money on healing myself and I eventually discovered my own abilities as a healer.

Becoming An Escort Was One of The Best Things I Ever Did

It was actually during this time that I stopped partying and I had the time to spend on doing personal development and building my current business. Escorting was a means for me to travel, pay for courses, and fund my other business ventures. What I didn't realise at the time was how much it would teach me about men and how it would lead me into helping men and then teaching other women and escorts about men! Doing escort work was always a part of my soul's calling, it just evolved over time as I came more into alignment with my own soul.

I believe this is contrary to the stereotypes that are out there about escorts. Because that's all they are—stereotypes. The sex workers I have come to know are some of the most intelligent and self-aware women I have had the pleasure of spending time with. Many of them have become close friends and clients of mine who are just like me and also passionate about helping people and are making a real difference in the world!

Blending Sex Work With Spirituality

So here I was now working both as a sex worker and a spiritual healer. Two professions that felt very different to each other. That was until I experienced my first tantric massage and realised that I could blend sexuality and spirituality together! It was like an inner knowing had just been remembered…like…OF COURSE sex and spirituality go together and how could I not have seen this before?

As I started on my own sexual healing journey I became obsessed about learning all I could about tantra and sacred sexuality. I would soon find myself creating tantric practices and sacred sex rituals to experience with my clients. I was slowly becoming more of a tantric escort and sexual healer, or what some may call a Sacred Sexual Priestess. I started to realise that I had this gift to initiate men. I was able to open men up to experiencing deeper connection with themselves. I was able to help them open their hearts through their sexuality. Some of these experiences were incredibly profound!

Men would come to see me for deep healing work, to heal their sexual issues, to open their minds and bodies to a whole new way of exploring their sexuality, to get their intimacy needs met in a healthy way through conscious touch practices, to have more sexual confidence, to heal erectile dysfunction and premature ejaculation, to heal porn or sex addiction, to become multi-orgasmic.

They also came to learn how to truly pleasure and give to a woman in a way that honours her and makes her feel safe. This also felt more honouring for me and my body too, as the men were no longer having sex in the way they wanted with me; it was now on my terms as I became their teacher and guide. I was amazed at how many men were really willing to work on themselves and become better lovers!

They would share their deepest desires, vulnerabilities, and the things they felt too ashamed to tell anyone else about. This is something they had done with me as a non-tantric escort too, but now I knew how to hold space for them so they felt safe to express themselves sexually and emotionally.

I started to see men in a whole new light. I felt so much compassion for them. I felt like I had found my true calling and now I just wanted to help others to love themselves and awaken like I had!

And then HE came into my life.

The Woundmate to Heal All Woundmates

This is when woundmate number 666 entered my life …*yes he felt like the devil!* … the one that would break me the fuck open so deeply to my own love, but not before bringing me down to the depths of my core wounds.

Let's call this woundmate Leo. He was so what I thought was "my type." Polynesian, broad shoulders, charismatic, funny, he spoke with a deep soulful voice, and the best part was that he was very keen on me and he also happened to be spiritual!

He fell in love with me almost immediately, so he said. Here I had gone from Mr False Twin Flame running away from me to Leo pouring his love all over me and into every crack and cranny he could find. He even told me that I was his "twin soul" on our first night together and that "he had missed me since our last life together," that he "felt so drawn to my amazing aura." Those words were melt worthy to me!

However there was a little niggling voice, a voice in the back of my head saying "something isn't quite right here." So when Leo asked me to be his girlfriend on that first night I told him that I needed more time. I also explained to him that I worked as an escort and that I wasn't willing to give up escorting to be with him so he needed to be very sure that he was okay with it. He said he was fine with it, but down the track I would find out that he really wasn't and that he would use this to manipulate me in the cruellest and most vindictive way.

Two weeks later he told me that he had fallen in love with me and that he had never been in love like this before. He said that I was his first true love, that he would love me until his last breath, and that I was his dream girl. He told me that I was the only woman that he had ever truly wanted to marry and he couldn't believe that someone like me would want to be with him.

These were all the words I had been longing to hear from a man and he was lathering them on me, which made me feel so wanted, loved, special, and adored. On top of that he seemed to be okay with the fact that I was an escort.

It sounded too good to be true.

IT WAS.

There Were So Many Red Flags

Although I wasn't in love with him in the same way, I told myself that it would just take me more time and that I should just give him a chance. I wanted to explore the connection and see what was there, so I ignored my intuition and I agreed to be his girlfriend. It seemed like he never wanted to leave my side and from that moment on we were attached at the hip.

I know now that him wanting to move so fast and lovebombing me with all those words were actually red flags of a narcissist. Back then, I had no idea what a narcissist was or that such a person even existed. I ignored many other red flags too such as the way he talked about his ex-partners.

He told me that they were all psychos, stalkers, cheaters, and liars. He told me his sob stories and although I listened with empathy, part of me really didn't like the way he spoke about them so badly. But it wasn't just them he spoke about from a place of blame, it was everyone and everything. It was always someone else's fault. It seemed that he was always the victim and never took responsibility for his actions.

I was blind to that red flag though and within a month we had moved in together and he left his job. He said he would easily get another job straight away—it never happened.

These were all huge signs of what was about to come for me.

I Chose Him Over Escorting

The day came when I got booked for an escort job. I had taken time off for the holidays and had only been doing tantric massage sessions up until about a month into the relationship. And then I got a call for an escort session. I knew this day would come. I spoke to Leo about it and he said something along the lines of "do whatever you want" and the tone it came across to me was as though he didn't really care. He would later tell me that I should have known that he wasn't okay, that I should have known better. I would late discover that he would use this to gaslight me, another narcissist's manipulation tactic that we will explore later in the book.

Instead of speaking of his discomfort with me, he left the hotel room whilst I saw the client. It was an awful session as I found it hard to be intimate with someone else; I even felt guilty. When Leo came back after the session he refused to sleep in the same bed with me; he made out like it was now dirty and he couldn't believe I would do that to him. Part of my response to this was "I'm doing it for us; now that you are not working, I have to support you too." I was resentful that I was getting punished for him not speaking his needs to me and trying to make me feel more guilty than I already did.

Little did I know then that my choice to see this client would now go on to be used in almost every single argument we had. He would always claim that "this all started right back when you chose to see that client; if you hadn't done that, then we wouldn't be fighting now."

From that moment on I would never win with him.

I was so confused. I thought he said I could do whatever I wanted! In that moment I knew I had to make a choice.

It was escorting or him.

I chose him. In doing so, not only did I give up escorting, but I gave up myself.

It Was Scary to Leave Escorting

It had always provided financial security for me, but I had also wanted to leave the industry for the last couple of years. I was building up my Tantra business so I could do that and one of the reasons I wanted to leave was so I could have a relationship. I had told myself a story that no man would want me while I was an escort, but realised later on that one of the reasons I was staying in the industry was to protect myself from building an emotional connection with a man for fear of getting hurt. Clearly that didn't work!

So I now had the relationship and I thought perhaps this was the universe giving me the push I needed?

Because He Was Spiritual I Did Not Suspect Him

Leo also considered himself to be quite spiritual; he meditated, had visions (apparently), and appeared quite empathetic and able to read and pick up on energy, and he did appear to have energy have healing abilities. He came to meditation classes with me and everyone seemed to love him! I looked like the luckiest girl to have a man who was charismatic, attractive, masculine, spiritual, and so in love with me.

Even if I knew about narcissists back then there is no way I would ever have thought he was a narcissist since he was so "spiritual."

Leo then decided that he wanted to learn tantric massage too and make it his career. So when he asked me to teach him, I thought it would be a wonderful way for him to channel his healing abilities. He said he felt really drawn to it and instead of getting a normal job, he wanted to live the lifestyle I lived. Since I worked from home, it meant being at home together A LOT. Every day, all the time. Being in each other's faces. Working together, eating together, playing together, doing almost everything together.

Initially he would go out of the apartment when I was seeing clients and then we decided that he would just stay in our bedroom. This is where he spent most of his time when I was working, playing around on Snapchat and Facebook. It would trigger me because I always felt like I was doing all the work and providing for us.

He would claim that he was researching Tantra, but I soon came to realise to never believe a word he said. He would only see one or two clients a week, so it was still me making most of the money and paying the bills, which now was a lot less than I was used to since I wasn't escorting anymore. I now had two people to support and half the income!

My resentment began to build.

I Caught Him Secretly Messaging His Ex-Girlfriend

What he also had failed to tell me was that he was still in contact with his ex-girlfriend and that they had still been seeing each other casually just before we got together. His messages to her were often nasty and abusive and he even would tell her how much better I was than her. He said it was all her, that she was just an energy vampire. I asked him to stop messaging her because it was affecting our relationship and he said he did. However, he continued contacting her secretly, but at the same time accusing me of connecting with other men behind his back whilst also telling me he has a boundary that I am not allowed to be in contact with my exes. This was of course a huge double standard - which became a regular ongoing occurrence.

The more suspicious I became of his lies, the more his accusations towards me became worse. He would go off at me at the smallest things, swearing and calling me nasty names, and even calling me by his ex's name. He would assume connections with my male friends were more than just friends and I would try to defend myself and give my power away trying to explain things because in my eyes I thought I had done nothing wrong!

The whole thing just seemed crazy to me, but apparently, according to him, I was the crazy one! But that was always his story when we got into a fight; he would say "all you women are the same, you are all liars, you are all cunts, you can't be trusted, you are just like my ex, you are a psycho, you are crazy, you have bi-polar."

I told myself that he was just triggered from his past and it had nothing to do with me and if he just did the healing work on himself we could make the relationship work.

But when I saw him hiding messages to his ex for the third time, I had enough. I made him move out that day.

But I made the big mistake of staying in contact with him. I reached out to make sure he was okay and three days later he had moved back in. He broke down in tears when he said he realised how much he loved me and didn't want to be without me and he then cut contact with her.

I thought that he really meant it.

I Became His Emotional Punching Bag

Now that he wasn't talking to and abusing her, he turned that anger towards me. I was literally his emotional punching bag. He started picking at me about everything. Telling me my beliefs were wrong and his were right. Making fun of my healing work and spiritual friends, calling me a fake and a fraud. It was like he found all my insecurities and deliberately stabbed me where it hurt. These were the things that at the beginning of the relationship I had vulnerably shared with him, when he had appeared to be such an attentive listener and wanted to know everything about me. He had come off so empathetic and caring. I didn't know that he only appeared that way so that he had fuel to use against me later.

It was a regular occurrence that at night when I went to bed he would stay up until all hours watching movies. When I asked him to come to bed for cuddles he would get triggered, throw his phone and call me nasty names. This eventually got worse and led to horrid physical abuse. The first time it ever got physical was one night when he threw a bag at me twice which hit me in the back. The next day he claimed that the bag didn't hit me, but that it "bounced off the bed head." I had bruises on my back that proved otherwise. This was just another form of him gaslighting me.

The next day I left the house and went away for a few days to clear my head. I wrote him a letter about how I was feeling and told him that if he wanted to continue this relationship he needed to do some serious healing on himself. I went into healer mode and told him all the things

I think he needed to do. He agreed to start working on healing himself when I got back.

But for the next couple of months the same thing kept happening, but the abuse got much, much worse. I wasn't functioning properly because I was kept up with the abuse to the early hours of the morning. I had to cancel clients and I had to turn down opportunities that would have furthered my career. I had been asked by an online spiritual TV show to come on the show and be a panelist, but I had to keep turning them down, telling them the time wasn't right. The truth was that I wasn't in any state to be talking about self-love when I felt so lost!

I would later on find out that he had blocked the producer's number on my phone to try and sabotage my success. He once told me that he was afraid I would forget about him if I became super successful, yet my drive was one of the things he loved about me when we first got together.

Why It Was So Hard to Leave Him

You may wonder why I just didn't leave him then? I wish it had been that easy. After almost every fight I would ask him to leave and he would say "I've got nowhere to go" or he would call his friends in front of me and play the poor-me card and tell them that I was kicking him out on the street.

He would make me out to be the nasty one.

He would appeal to my empathetic nature. He would apologise and tell me that I didn't deserve to be treated this way, that he couldn't believe he was acting this way towards me.

And the worst line of all was "I think I abuse you because I love you so much."

He was right, I did deserve better. But my empathetic nature wasn't going to just leave him on the street. I suggested he could stay with his family and friends, but there were always excuses as to why that wouldn't work, mostly that he didn't want to be a burden to anyone, again, playing the victim.

Then there were the deaths in his family. Three people in his family passed away whilst we were together, including his brother. Leo had also told me that he had tried to kill himself just before we met. He said that meeting me it was like an angel had saved him and now he felt alive and happy again. Because of this I was afraid of what he might to himself do if I left him.

Then Came All the Threats

The other thing that made it hard to leave was that he was constantly threatening me. He threatened that if I left or told anyone about the abuse, that "it would be war." The look in his eyes when he said this was like a demon; there was no doubt in my mind that he meant it.

He became extremely vindictive at times and would record me screaming and crying on his phone and threaten to post it on Facebook so that "people could see what I was really like."

He would say "look at how angry and upset you are, you are not a healer, you are a fraud." He also said things about our relationship to his friends that were twisted to make him appear to be the victim and me out to be this terrible girlfriend.

He then threatened that if I left him he would publicly post on Facebook that I had worked as an escort. He knew how much I didn't want that to happen. Even though I knew I would go public with my story one day, it had to be on my terms when I was ready, not from it being used as a form of manipulation to keep me trapped in an abusive relationship.

There was a part of me that did want to say "fuck it, I don't care, just do it."

I Completely Shut Myself Down

When I tried to leave the house during our fights he threatened to smash up my phones and laptop because it had all my work and my book writing on it which he knew was extremely precious to me. This led to him taking my phones and car keys off me and pinning me down on the bed so I couldn't move anywhere and then locking me inside the bedroom. When I tried to scream he would cover my mouth and hold me down harder, sit on top of me, and threaten to bash me up if the police came knocking on the door, so that in his words "he will have something to go to jail for." He didn't seem afraid of the police.

I completely shut myself down. I stopped expressing myself. I was afraid that anything I shared with him would be turned around on me. I couldn't be vulnerable with him anymore. He had now gone from punching his phone and throwing things at me to punching holes in doors. He would laugh and say "now you better fix it." Most of my money started to go into getting things fixed that he had broken in his rage outs.

And then began the choking, smacking, suffocating, pushing down pillows and wrapping blankets over my head, whacking me, hair pulling, slapping, spitting on me, and all whilst laughing at me and saying nasty things. At one point he said he felt like hanging me. If I tried to resist or escape he would just pull me back on the bed and sit on top of me again and hurt me more. If I kept my mouth shut and lay there still, he would just provoke me until I said something or physically hurt me enough until I tried to push him off. It's like he wanted me to fight him, as though he got off on it.

I Felt So Trapped

My life was no longer a life of freedom where I was building my career and travelling to Bali for retreats. My daily life was managing whatever I could do to not trigger him. Making sure that I said and did the things that were the least likely to lead to abuse. I was walking on eggshells constantly.

The Woundmate Experience

I had to be careful of the words I used, because he would twist anything I said into something to use against me. I would pray that none of my male friends would message me, because that would completely set him off. I was not even able to message my friends or family about what was going on because he would go through my phone when I was asleep and read everything I sent and received.

Only two friends knew about some of what I was experiencing, but they had no idea how bad it really was. I felt too ashamed to reach out and tell anyone and I didn't want to keep lying so I stopped talking to most of my friends. I was avoiding speaking to my family who lived overseas, because I didn't want to have to lie to them.

I even went quiet on social media. Everyone always thought I was so inspirational, but now I felt like I was slowly dying on the inside. I had nothing inspirational to say.

The whole concept of having the freedom to do what I want, when I wanted became so foreign to me. I wondered if I would ever be free to just be myself again.

The Sex Literally Became Lifeless

One night after he had been pinning me down on the bed, yet again, he decided he wanted to have sex. I thought to myself that it was easier to just let him do it rather than trying to fight it. I felt like it was a choice between the physical violence and the sex. His energy was different when it came to the sex, it was much softer, it was so much better than his uncontrollable rage monster. I knew that if I fought him about the sex, it would set his rage off.

So even though I said no, I didn't try to physically fight him off. I certainly was in no way into it. I just lay there like a lifeless body as he slowly pulled open my legs. I kept saying in a calm voice, "I don't want to do this." But he didn't listen and he kept going, until eventually he was inside of me.

I tensed up my whole body and vagina to try and numb myself so I couldn't feel anything. Tears were welling up in my eyes and when he tried to kiss me I turned my head away. I had never felt so disgusted by him.

I then turned to him and said, "How does it feel to have sex with a lifeless body? Because that's all I am right now."

It felt like my soul had left my body as I disassociated from it. I couldn't feel anything, no pain or pleasure. It was like I wasn't even there, I just lay there completely frozen. He ignored me and kept going.

It wasn't until the next day when I was telling my friend about it that she said to me with empathy and sadness in her voice, "Oh, honey, you know that was rape?" I hadn't seen it like that. A part of me thought that because he was my partner it was like he had a right to have sex with me whether I wanted it or not; I guess I didn't want to see it like that. But she was right, he had sex without my consent and this was rape.

When I spoke to him later on about it, his response was "you should have kept your legs shut then" and then he turned it back on me and suggested a time when I had done the same thing to him; like there was ever a time I would have forced myself on him!

But his comment did make me question myself and if I had done something like that to him, again, just more gaslighting.

The Day I Found a Hidden Camera

There was one unforgettable day where I had just started a tantric massage session and something felt off. My psychic senses were ringing, all I kept hearing in my ear was "there is a camera in here." Sure enough, after having a quick scan of the room, I spied something black sitting just behind the blind. It was his GoPro and he was watching me from the next room!

I was absolutely fuming. How could he do this? He claimed he put it in there for my safety and so he could watch me and learn more about how I do tantric massage. I knew the real reason he had it in there was so he could keep an eye on me.

It Was Like I Was Dating Two Different People

What was confusing for me the most is that it wasn't all bad because outside of the abuse we actually we had a lot of special and romantic times together. We took long strolls on the beach, holding hands, stopping to kiss when the sun was going down with the water playfully at our feet, dinners out, romantic pool swims, he would give me massages, tell me how amazing I was, and he would even clean the house and do my washing! He often came to meditation groups, healing workshops, and volunteered helping the homeless, so I felt that he was showing me that he was a good person that wanted to work on himself. Often the day after an abusive episode he would offer to give me a massage and we would be back to being all loved up again.

It was so hard to believe that he could be two very different people. This incredibly romantic loved-up version of him is who I thought must have been the real him and that the abusive version of him was just coming from the pain of his past relationships. I thought if he just healed from his past and stopped projecting it on me, then we could work! I just wanted to help him be the man that I knew he could be and not function from his pain. I thought I was going to be the woman that helped him to heal!

I Was So Torn Between Leaving and Trying To Make It Work

By this stage I was feeling all kinds of emotions, and I was constantly torn between thoughts of trying to find a way to leave him in the safest way to then thinking that if we both just healed ourselves then maybe we could work. The abuse made me want to leave and then the next day would make me want to work it out; it was a constant mental battlefield and emotional rollercoaster.

I even went to psychics looking for answers and none of them told me to leave him. I even had one tell me that we would get married and move to America, have kids together, and live happily ever after! So I stayed and kept trying.

But it was my own intuition that I needed to trust, that was one of the biggest lessons that I would have to learn from this. And in my heart of hearts I knew that this relationship wasn't right. So why was it so damn hard for me to leave?!

His Remorse Gave Me Hope

Eventually the neighbours heard us fighting and called the police. When they arrived, they separated us, sat me down, and asked me what had happened. I froze. I didn't know what to say. All I could think was *he has children, I cannot do this to them, I cannot let their father go to jail.*

I had seen how much he appeared to love his kids and I just couldn't leave them without their dad around. I told myself that he was just going through such a hard time right now with all the deaths in his family and this isn't really him. I knew he would calm down tomorrow and everything would be okay again.

So I didn't tell them about the abuse and they left. It did, however, defuse the situation and he did have a lot of remorse the next day. He swore on his kids' lives that he would never hurt me again. He cried, told me how much he loved me, and gave me lots of cuddles.

But then it happened a second time. I was crying this time when the police came and I told them that he had taken my phone and thrown it out the door. This was enough information for the police to put a domestic violence order on him. That's when we finally decided to move out of the house and go our separate ways a few weeks later.

Another Woman Came Into the Picture

Once we had both moved out I felt like a huge weight had been lifted. I felt so free!

I was free – for all of a week.

Again, we made the mistake of staying in contact.

Then we saw each other again; yes, I know, again, right?!

Why did I keep doing this to myself? It was like we were addicted to each other and just could not stay away! This addiction is what I know now is called trauma bonding, which makes it so hard to stay away from the abuser.

The abuse, of course, happened again and we broke up, again.

And then he met someone else four days later, who, according to him, was an escort who was younger, more attractive, and more successful than me. He was sending me photos of her giving him a lap dance in her lingerie, like it was just some joke to him. Those photos messed me up big time.

I got so triggered I started acting like a crazy person! I even got in my car and decided I was going to drive to see him and stop this. I started to drive and then I revved up the car and hit the brakes and turned back around. I didn't actually want to drive to him, but I wanted him to think that I did so that he would stop being with her. I wanted him to care more about me. I wanted him to choose me!

This was triggering deep wounds for me around other women and he knew this. He knew this would upset me and so he was doing it deliberately to trigger me. But I didn't know that at the time. Looking back now I don't even know if those photos were real or if he just took them from Snapchat and made the whole thing up!

You see I didn't know back then that so much of what he was doing was just to trigger me to get narcissistic supply, I thought it was all true. I didn't even think someone would go to the lengths of making so much stuff up just to trigger me. But once I knew he was narcissistic, I could see how much of it he actually completely made up!

The Violence Became Even Worse

Whilst all of this was happening I had just gone back to escort work. Now that we weren't together anymore, I was like I can do whatever I want and he doesn't need to know. Besides, he was now seeing this other woman who was an escort anyway and they had already had tantric sex (according to him), which he then later told me he lied about. The next time he contacted me I had seen four escort clients. This is when he told me that he had now started going to counselling and attending an anger management course.

I was so happy to hear that and he came to see me and told me about everything he had been learning from his sessions. He said he still wanted to be with me and he didn't even care about the other woman. I could see all the work he was now doing and I thought maybe this time things would be different!

I couldn't bear the thought of him being with someone else, especially now he was doing all this work; it wouldn't be fair that she would get to have the new, improved version of him!

So I stopped escorting and we got back together.

But I didn't tell him about seeing those clients, because I knew it would set him off into a jealous rage. He was suspect though and I caved a week later and told him the truth.

Big mistake.

The violence started … yet again. And it got even worse.

The Threats Became Real

Now the threats of breaking my personal property became real. Deliberately ripping my necklaces off when he was choking me and then trying to force feed me one of the pendants, holding my nose and mouth shut to make me swallow it.

Fights in the car led to him smashing the radio and windscreen, pulling off parts and driving recklessly. He would threaten to drive us into a wall and would deliberately swerve into the side of the road to scare me. Almost every time he drove it was like being on a real rollercoaster ride; I went into panic and feared for my life many times.

I had to keep replacing my phones as he smashed five of them and this really affected my business. He smashed my massage table, my speakers, my spare laptop, and my laptop screen. I stopped wearing jewellery and buying anything new for myself and I starting hiding valuable items for fear he would break them.

He Deliberately Used Other Women to Trigger Me

For the next three months our relationship was very on and off. He would get into a violent rage, then he would talk to the counsellor, things would be great, and then he would become abusive again. If I tried to end things he would go straight to the other woman. Let's call her Kristen for the sake of this story.

He would phone her and tell her that I was acting crazy and being abusive towards him and that he wanted to leave me and come and see her right in front of me. He would say really nasty things about me to her whilst he had locked me in the bedroom with no phone and nowhere to get out and no way to get help.

Kristen would empathise with him, only because, of course, she too had been sucked into the lovebombing phase of his narcissism and his "poor me" story. He was so believable. She was only another form of narcissistic supply and he was playing us off against each other. This is called triangulation. He would go constantly back and forth between us. When things weren't going well with me, he would go to her, and he knew that when he went to her I would want to take him back.

There were many other women too; he would say they were just his friends and I was worrying about nothing, but they would send selfies, sexy photos, and flirty texts to each other and talk about how they wanted to sleep with him. He had me so convinced that I actually started to question whether I was jumping to conclusions and sexy selfies were "normal" things that just friends do.

But if I ever received just a simple text from another man, who was definitely only a friend, he would always assume that there was something more going on and it would end in a war! He even admitted once at a workshop that if I was doing what he was doing with women with other men then it would be over and he even saw and admitted that he had double standards and was being a hipocrite.

I Started To Think I was The Crazy one

Every time we got into a fight and he got onto the phone to another woman it would trigger me like crazy. He even started deliberately getting on the phone to other women because he knew it would trigger me; he once admitted that's why he did it.

Then I actually began to act crazy! As soon as he got on the phone I would run to the balcony and would half hop over it, threatening that if he left to go to her that I would kill myself. This only added more fuel to his argument about me being crazy! A few times I even physically hurt myself in front of him, such as hitting and scratching myself, and at one point I hit myself over the head with a frying pan.

Often times I would be lying in the floor in fear and he would be kicking me and laughing at me calling me an idiot. I was fuming with so much rage and anger for how he was treating me.

The Woundmate Experience

I was so lost. I was so confused. I was so not myself.

Who was this crazy person I had now become? This behavior was totally out of character for me, I had never acted this way in my entire life!

He told me that I should see a counsellor too, so I did and she told me no wonder I was acting this way with his behavior and me being responsible for everything. When I told him what she said, he told me that my counsellor sounded like an idiot and that she was wrong. This just ended up in more violence towards me.

It was all just one giant, sadistic game to him and he got off on it.

It was like he was playing a game called "how much can I trigger EJ and make her act crazy today?"

He had identified my deepest insecurities and wounds. His mission was to attack them so he could turn it all around on me, so that he could say that I was the crazy one. It was working.

I actually started to wonder "am I the crazy one?"

All of this was giving him narcissistic supply. (I'll be explaining more about what narcissistic supply is in chapter 9).

He Secretly Recorded Me Having Sex

He had put the camera back in my work room again and although he told me he couldn't record from his GoPro to his phone I would soon find out that he had found a way. He began to text me during my sessions and started telling me what to do.

One day he said,

"I think you should have sex with this guy."

He had now gone from raging out at me for seeing that one client when we first got together and the four whilst we were broken up to now telling me that I should escort again!

But it was only with men he approved of and he now told me it was a turn-on to see me having sex with another man.

I was resistant to doing it at first only because I was afraid of how he might twist it around later and use it against me. But because of how much being in this relationship had affected my work and finances, we really needed the money. I ended up seeing four escort clients with his approval.

Then one day we were both scrolling through photos on his computer and suddenly there was a shot of me and one of the clients I had sex with. It was a full video of me and my client! He had downloaded a recording app so that he could record it. I was so shocked. Although you would think by this time that nothing would surprise me with his behavior!

He took it like it was just a silly joke and deleted it. But it was not a joke to me. I couldn't do this anymore. Enough was enough. How much torture was I going to put myself through?

I Devised a Cunning Plan to Leave for Good

I now knew that the only reason I was staying was because there was another woman in the picture and it was triggering my betrayal wounds and story of not being chosen. If she wasn't in the picture I would have left him months ago.

I had also started to discover the massive amount of blatant lies he had told me from the start. He was constantly changing his stories now and I had become extremely suspicious. It would start to do my head in trying to work out what was real and what was not and I was questioning my own beliefs and morals.

Eventually I just assumed he was lying all the time and I just couldn't be bothered arguing with him about it. He would always claim that I was the liar and in his twisted mind, I think that's how he really saw it. I was now bored with the relationship and the connection was dead since it wasn't safe for me to be vulnerable.

And I did end up lying to him and hiding many things from him mainly to protect myself from his abusive and manipulative reactions. I mostly lied about being in contact with male friends when we were broken up, because I knew he would twist it around in his mind that it was more than that, like he had done previously. I had to also keep deleting messages when reaching out for help from my friends.

And then there was the secret plan I started to devise to leave him.

Finally, after I had enough of my soul being destroyed and myself and my personal property being smashed to pieces, I set up to leave so I wouldn't be able to go back …EVER AGAIN.

I Had to Take Drastic Measures to Leave Safely

Many times I had asked him for time apart so I could get back to being myself again, but he always said that for him, time apart meant breaking up for good. Which is funny to look back on now, since we actually had plenty of break-ups, time apart, and then got back together!

It was just another way to control me.

I just had to devise a plan to leave in a way that meant I could never go back. I knew I had to do something drastic. Something that meant he would never want to be with me again, where I did not have a choice about it. I knew I had to be super sneaky about this so he would not find out what I was doing and try to stop me or threaten me.

My plan was to go to Melbourne and do a Tantra retreat. I knew that one of the reasons I kept going back to him was because I hated the feeling of being alone. So spending a week in a community of supportive people was exactly what I needed to be around when I left.

I knew I had to go away to somewhere we couldn't meet up in person. I also worked out that financially if I didn't end up going I would lose over $2,000 and I wasn't willing to lose that much money. I calculated that I needed to leave him a week before the retreat so I could make enough money for the trip.

September 6 would be the last day that I could leave him. If I didn't leave him then I would have lost that chance, lost that money, and all my planning would have been for nothing.

I will never forget that date. That was the day my life would change forever. I was counting down the days.

I Discovered That He Had Been Escorting Too

In the lead up to September 6 my mind was still going back and forth about leaving. That was until we had another incident with the police and he almost ended up in jail.

That night we had a fight over him using my internet to download music; it was a silly fight that ended up with him throwing all the raw chicken I was cooking over the floor and walls. The Police wanted to take him away, but instead I minimised what happened.

After the Police left he rang a female friend of his and told her from a victimised perspective how I had now slept with nine men whilst we were together and that he had a recording of it on his computer that he had now uploaded to the cloud.

He also forgot to mention to her (and to me) that he had also been escorting. That's right, all the time he had been going off at me for escorting, he had been doing it himself, once with my knowledge and I don't know how many times without!

Leo and I had previously talked about him doing escorting, but he always said it wasn't really for him and that he "wasn't that type of person" or that he could only get his cock hard with someone he loved. However, I found out from other escorts in my community that he had been messaging them about helping him become an escort and he even told them that he was the one that taught me tantric massage, making himself out to be some kind of tantric massage teacher!

I didn't know if he was genuinely messaging them or if he was actually doing it because he knew it would get back to me and it would trigger me.

The funny thing was that I would have been completely fine with him escorting. I always saw escort work as being very separate to my personal sex life, although by this stage the two had started to blend with his controlling ways and me allowing it.

The way I ended up finding out about his escorting was that one of his past client's husband came to see me for a tantric massage and told me that Leo had sex with his wife at a time when we were still together.

So much for "I'm just not that type of person" and "I can only get hard with someone I love." He had been making me wrong for escorting, when he had been doing it all along. This was more gaslighting so I would never suspect him.

Getting Ready for the Big Day

He knew something was up with me because he bought me flowers and went grocery shopping for the first time ever! None of his usual devaluing tactics were working, so he was trying to lovebomb me again (I will share more on what this is in chapter 13).

It was September 5; tomorrow was the big day. We had been staying at his sister's house for the weekend, which I thought was the perfect place for me to leave him. Firstly, because I knew this was a place he would be less likely to abuse me because she had kids and secondly, because I thought he would be okay there with his sister once I left.

I had already told him that I was leaving to go up to work two hours north tomorrow, but that I wasn't sure if I wanted him to come with me. Whilst I was still deciding he was trying to convince me to take him with me and that he would really be different this time … yada yada … same shit, different day!

I had organised it so that all my belongings were completely packed up in my car which was sitting in the driveway. I wanted to be able to just hop in it and drive away without him breaking anything!

It was all set up so perfectly.

Yet, I still had doubts. A part of me still wondered if we could make it work, especially since he had been so nice the last few days; it was like finally he had turned a corner and was seeing the light! But I had felt this way before, many times.

I knew that I had made this plan too good not to back out of it. There was too much at stake to risk not doing it.

I knew that if he came with me that next day, I wouldn't make the money that I needed to go to Melbourne and that I would never end up at the retreat. I would lose that money and I would stay in this repetitive cycle with him. I had made going to Melbourne far more worth it than staying with him. This was my best chance.

I Made the Choice That Would Change My Life Forever

The next day I told him. I told him I was leaving without him, that it was over, and this time I actually meant it.

He went into his usual rage, as I expected, and I got into my car and drove out of the driveway and around the block.

I was freeeeeeeee!

The Woundmate Experience

And then I stopped.

I felt sad. I realised that this would be the last time I would ever see him.

I turned around.

I drove back in. I went back up to the house and knocked on the door. I can't even remember what I said. I didn't know why I was doing this. I couldn't seem to help myself. I was going to completely ruin my plan!

What the hell was I doing?

He was fuming, locked the door on me and refused to talk to me; I'll never forget the demonic look on his face staring at me through the window.

Seeing that side of him in that moment, was actually the best thing for me. I shakily went back to my car. I sat in the driver's seat, pulled out my phone and I did the only thing I know I could do in that moment - I rang my best friend.

Thank God she answered my call.

I told her that part of me wanted to leave and part of me wanted to go back inside and smooth things over and make it all okay again. I felt so stuck. In my heart of hearts I knew I had to leave. I knew that this was it. So why was I struggling to just drive away and never look back?

She asked me some questions and she took me through a healing process which helped me to see the wound of "I am not wanted" which had kept being triggered for me in this relationship.

As I sat there going through this process with her I cried and cried.

Yes, that was it!

Every time he was going to the other woman it made me feel that he didn't want me, but when I would take him back then I was just trying to feel like he did want me and prove that he would choose me over her.

I had massive wounds around other women and not being wanted and that along with the trauma bonds were keeping me in this toxic situation.

Once I got off the phone, I knew what I had to do.

I turned the key of the ignition. I slowly drove off.

And I drove and I drove and I drove… and I never looked back.

I WAS FINALLY FREE!

It Was Time to Heal From the Abuse

I now had to choose who I was going to be in the face of this break-up. I could choose to shut down, numb, take on more beliefs about men being abusers and liars, or do what I used to do, date other men to avoid feeling the pain.

Or I could choose to look inside myself and acknowledge the part of me that feels used and abused and hold myself through it. I could choose to use my experience to take a stand for myself and for any man or woman who goes through abuse.

My real place of power in all of this has been to own my part in it and not be the victim in the story so it won't repeat for me, or for generations to come.

What we choose to do with the pain after we end a relationship is a defining moment of how it will affect our lives and future relationships.

Here's to September 6—the first day I really chose to love me first.

The day I started to become the one.

The Woundmate Experience

The Stigma of Sex Work Needs to End

I feel to also mention here that the stigma of sex work often effects worker's lives and relationships. This happens to the point where many have been threatened, manipulated and abused by their partners, family members, friends and other people. This has put them in dangerous positions where they often don't feel safe to say anything or reach out for support. It's time that this stigma ends and that sex work is seen as a normal job just like any other.

Sex work is one of the best jobs I have ever had. If it wasn't for this work, I wouldn't be where I am today and I wouldn't be helping men and women in the way I do now. I will be forever grateful for my time as an escort, all that I learned and all the incredible connections I made. I know it was always meant to be part of my purpose and journey.

I want all sex workers to be given the same rights and respect as other professions.

For this reason I hold the red umbrella on the cover of my book with pride because it is the International Symbol of Sex Worker Rights.

I hope my story will bring more awareness to this issue.

Chapter 3

Maturing the Masculine to Hold the Healthy Feminine

"When a woman's inner masculine is fully present to hold her, she feels safe to surrender to love"

Before I take you through the journey of how I healed myself from the abuse, I want to use this chapter to explain masculine and feminine more clearly, as I will use these terms throughout the book.

In the introduction you heard me use terms like inner masculine and feminine. I want to make it clear what I mean by this because masculine and feminine terms are thrown around a lot these days without really knowing what they actually mean.

'"You have to be more feminine" or "You are not feminine enough!"'

I used to hear this all the time when I first started on my spiritual healing journey.

I was like "okay, tell me what I need to do and I'll do whatever it takes!"

I would attend divine feminine awakening embodiment workshops and I would really try so hard to be more feminine, and although a lot of it really helped me embody my feminine energy I would always keep going back to being in my immature masculine, particularly when it came to how I was relating to men!

It wasn't until I attended a retreat with the International School of Temple Arts (ISTA) that I discovered that not only did I need to work on being feminine, but I also needed to work on maturing my inner masculine energy.

I already thought I had my masculine energy down pat so I didn't really need any work in that area.

Oh boy, that could not have been further from the truth!

My inner masculine energy was more like a scared little boy! What my feminine really needed was for him to be mature, grounded, and present to hold her and make her feel safe enough to open and flourish. Until my inner masculine matured she was not going to feel safe enough to be in her full power and radiance.

Up until this point I only thought there was masculine and feminine energy but what ISTA taught me was that there is the immature masculine, the mature masculine, the wounded feminine, and the healthy feminine. Similar teachings also call this the destructive or distorted masculine and feminine and the sacred masculine and divine feminine.

There is then also the light and dark masculine and the light and dark feminine. What I had been journeying with was only the light feminine energy and what I needed to do was to access more of the dark feminine where my rage, anger and deep grief was sitting and wanting to be felt and expressed.

We All Hold These Energies

If you are not aware of masculine and feminine energies, the main teaching behind this is that every person holds these.

It's not that man is masculine or woman is feminine, it is that we have both within us, and at times we will be in our masculine and at other times we will be in our feminine, and it's just knowing when to be in each energy, particularly when relating to others.

As you heal the relationship you have with men and women, you are effectively healing the relationship you have with your own inner masculine and inner feminine. The reverse is also true - if you heal your relationship with your inner masculine and feminine you will heal your relationships with men and women and this is effectively what this book is helping you to do. Because it's all a reflection.

This isn't a book that gives you feminine practices to help you be more feminine, but the healing you will do will create the trust and safety within you that is actually needed for you to step into more your healthy feminine power and vulnerability. Both men and women need to do this.

So what is being suggested here is that we have unevolved and evolved versions of these energies and the more we evolve them the healthier relationships we will have.

Healing the Relationship With Your Inner Masculine

From what I've experienced and seen is that the men who were showing up in my life in what appeared to be an immature and unhealthy way were actually reflecting back to me the relationship I had with my own inner masculine.

Here is how I was showing up in immature masculine energy:

I was always needing to be in control of everything in my life; I felt like I had to do everything myself; I was constantly rescuing and overgiving in relationships; I didn't trust myself or others; I was overly responsible; I had suppressed anger; I would avoid feeling my emotions and numb and distract myself; I didn't always trust or follow my intuition; I was very indecisive and needed to logically weigh things up; I was functioning more from fear than from love; I had low self-worth and was often in self-doubt; I would seek approval through my achievements; I was not present or grounded in my body; I was often all up in my head, overthinking and analysing things; I was always keeping myself busy doing something rather than just being present in the moment.

And then I was expecting a man to fully show up for me in his maturity and presence?!

Yeah, right, like that was going to happen!

If I wanted to attract healthy, mature men into my life, my inner masculine had A LOT of growing up to do!

The immature masculine energy is the one that appears to run the world. This can be a very destructive energy and is often fearful and distrustful. They will often take advantage of others to get their needs met. They may brag, show off, and intimidate others because underneath they have low self-worth.

Obviously I wasn't running all of these behaviours and I also had some mature masculine traits too, such as being goal focused, and driven. I was self-confident in some areas of my life and ultimately focused on unity rather than separation.

To Trust a Man Again, I Had to Trust My Inner masculine

The biggest disconnect though was that I wasn't fully feeling my emotions or being vulnerable. I was shut down. I wasn't in my heart. I was disconnected from my body and I was all up in my head most of the time. I was doing almost everything from a place of needing to achieve to prove my worth and constantly trying to prove that I was lovable.

My immature masculine was there protecting me and keeping me safe from getting hurt again. He was like an overprotective Father who wasn't letting his little girl run free!

So the journey to maturity had to begin with my willingness to feel the past hurt that was causing the shut down and disconnection from my heart and body.

For me to feel safe to feel again, I had to know that my inner masculine had me.

I had to know that he was there, fully showing up for me, fully present.

I had to know that he would speak up for me, that he would set healthy boundaries, honour his integrity, and make a strong decision to walk away from anything that did not serve me.

If I ever wanted to be able to trust a man again, I had to first build trust with my own inner masculine.

I had to trust my inner masculine to be there and hold me when I fell.

To not protect me from a place of fear, but to protect me like a divine father would, with loving presence.

Reclaiming Your Feminine Power

When I say "feminine power" some people may think of feminism. Although feminism served a great purpose at the time, it actually came from a more masculine form of power.

Because a feminine form of power is much more sensitive and gentle and her power actually lies in her vulnerability.

The healthy feminine energy is one where she is willing to show up and share, feel, and fully express herself and her feelings.

When she expresses her emotions they do not come from a place of needing to assert power or by projecting anger, but from a raw, authentic place of vulnerability. She gives herself permission to feel all her emotions - rage, anger, sadness and grief and she holds herself through it.

She is owning her pain, owning her story, and asking to be heard, willing to ask for support without expectations or neediness.

And she is fully open to receive help, to receive that support, to receive love.

She is caring, nurturing, and giving, but not from a place of needing to prove her worth, from an authentic place of love, compassion, and kindness.

She is deeply trusting and patient. When her inner masculine is present to hold her she feels safe to surrender to life and to surrender to love.

She is connected to her intuition and tapped into her creative life force.

She is a sensual being and owns her sexuality as her life force. She is incredibly courageous and intrinsically knows her worth in the world.

She lets go of the need to constantly be doing and instead leans back into her receptivity, into her being-ness.

You can always tell a woman who is in her feminine power because she completely radiates.

Men in the Wounded Feminine and Emasculation

This kind of feminine power lies inside both men and women. So when men evolve the relationship with their inner masculine, they will be able to access this expression of themselves more easily, which tends to be more challenging for men due to their conditioning.

Men need to feel safe to express the feminine part of themselves too, but what I am commonly seeing in western culture is that men are now more in their wounded feminine energy and women are more in their immature masculine energy and then they polarise back and forth between the two energies, especially in co-dependent relationships.

A woman will tend to go into her immature masculine energy when she doesn't feel safe, especially if that woman has experienced abuse.

They go into this energy to protect themselves and in the process they may unconsciously emasculate men.

Emasculation in this instance begins when a woman doesn't see a man for who he really is and this is mostly because the woman is running disempowering stories about men that she has created from society and her previous painful and unsafe experiences. It also comes from cultural conditioning and wounds passed down from previous generations.

Alison Armstrong in the book *The Queen's Code* suggests that women often assume that men are misbehaving when they don't act like a woman would. This is when a woman may energetically cut the man's balls off with her words and behaviour!

We are going to dive more into understanding emasculation later in this book.

Now it is certainly not women's fault that men are being emasculated, as men are being emasculated by society because they are not taught what it means to be a man in the modern world. They are no longer needed to hunt and provide for a woman and so it's become somewhat confusing for many men as to what their role is. They even often feel shame just for being a man.

After working intimately with thousands of men, I have grown to have so much compassion for them.

I've also seen men become "nice guys" to avoid being seen as an asshole or being seen as a sexual predator. Then they end up people pleasing for approval, not having healthy boundaries and even becoming resentful towards women when they overgive and feel unappreciated. This is when they may go into playing the victim role and find themselves getting hurt, walked on or used by women (usually ones in immature masculine energy). This is also similer for women who play the good girl role who want to avoid being seen as the bitch (myself included in this one!).

A Man's Vulnerability is Deeply Inspiring

The thing that saddens me the most is that men have been conditioned to suppress their emotions and taught that it's "weak" to show their vulnerability. But for me their vulnerability is actually what makes me feel safe as a woman to be vulnerable with them. It deeply inspires me when a man feels safe to be vulnerable with me!

Emasculation isn't just towards men either as women also emasculate themselves and their own masculine energy and men also emasculate themselves and essentially if a man feels emasculated he needs to look at where he is doing this to himself and where he is allowing it to be done to him! So the responsibility here is for each of us as individuals to heal our relationship with the masculine energy.

The wounded feminine energy is when there is depression, disconnection, manipulation, drama, insecurities, self-sabotage, impatience, a need for attention, neediness, gossiping, feeling unattractive, criticising of self and others, feelings of being trapped, putting expectations on others, blaming others, playing the victim, being a doormat, and being people pleasers.

I bet you can see a bit of these ones in yourself too, huh?

Even though I had been more in my immature masculine energy in my life, I definitely had been in my wounded feminine too!

> **#LOVETIP: MEN AND HEALTHY MASCULINITY**
>
> There is some great men's work being done around the world. The Mankind Project is a pioneer for this. If you are a man reading this or a woman who wants to support the men in your life to heal and grow please share this information with them. I highly recommend all men to get along to one of their men's groups and New Warrior trainings. You can find their website in the resources section at the back of this book.
>
> I also recommend both men and women watch the movie *The Mask You Live In* which is a documentary on Netflix sharing how the cultural definition of masculinity is harming boys and men.

When Polarity Feels Like Chemistry

Let's take a look at how these energies play out in relationships and how this shows up as chemistry and attraction.

Have you ever had an uncontrollable pull towards someone that you couldn't explain?

This is called - POLARITY

Polarity in this instance is two opposing energies, such as masculine and feminine that become magnetised to each other. What I discovered was that with most of my ex-partners I had been more in an immature masculine energy when I was playing the rescuer and they were more in a wounded feminine energy playing the victim.

This meant these energies were polarising each other and this created a magnetic pull between us. This felt like chemistry and attraction, which then became super addictive!

Having polarity with someone is awesome for creating sexual chemistry. This is why often the people you have the best sex with might be the worst ones for you!

When you know someone is not healthy for you but you say "oh, but the sex is so good!"

Yep—that's polarity.

What happens is that all the immature and unhealthy parts of each other that are not evolved and owned yet will be shown to us through this polarity. This is where you start to trigger each other, because these parts are being shown to you through the trigger and they are wanting to be seen and loved.

> **#LOVEBOMB: EVOLVING BOTH ENERGIES**
>
> If you only work on evolving your masculine or feminine energy, then generally you will end up in the immature or wounded energies. You really can't evolve one without also working on evolving the other!
>
> This is what I was doing when I was "trying to be more feminine" without actually evolving my masculine too. So ideally what you want to happen, is that you become an integrated being rather than being masculine or feminine (which are really only labels anyway).

Becoming an Integrated Being

When I decided to marry myself I saw that as having an inner marriage where I was marrying my inner masculine and feminine together and integrating them into more wholeness.

Essentially what I am taking you through in this book are a series of tools and practices to help you keep evolving and integrating your masculine and feminine energies to a mature and healthy place. The self-marriage ceremony is a way for you to integrate all that you have evolved over the course of the book. You don't need to do the ceremony to become integrated, but it certainly is a powerful ceremony that will help your journey.

I see an integrated being as one who owns all parts of themselves. Rather than projecting, disowning, or shaming their immature or wounded part of themselves they have a real willingness to look inside themselves, to own their triggers, and to see that these are showing them parts of themselves to be loved.

They are living more from their soul and heart space rather than functioning from a role or identity that they have created to keep themselves safe. They choose to love whatever arises, especially that which has been judged as wrong or bad.

They are committed to learning to love all of themselves and having that reflect out to the world.

They are committed to living from their healthy feminine and mature masculine energies, but they are not hard on themselves when they may deter from this, practising self-compassion and knowing that they are still only human after all!

Most of all they are committed to honouring, loving, valuing, and respecting themselves, knowing that everything that shows up for them in their relationships is simply a reflection of the relationship they have with their inner being and showing them where they are out of alignment.

From this place is where you feel more balanced and whole. You are not so much looking to get your needs met from other people and you are not constantly playing out old wounds or creating attraction with people that aren't healthy for you.

> **#LOVEBOMB: HEALTHY ATTRACTION**
>
> The more you evolve and heal your own energies the more you will find that your attraction changes towards certain people. With people that you used to feel a strong pull towards, you may wonder why you were ever attracted to them in the first place, because that past polarity just won't be there.
>
> If you are in a relationship with someone and you are both moving into being integrated the idea is then to create polarity between you. This where you consciously explore going in and out of the evolved masculine and feminine energies to create healthy polarity and sexual chemistry, rather than having attraction come from a wounded polarity.

So to put it simply, wounded polarity is when people are magnetically unexplainably pulled to each other because they are coming from the immature masculine and wounded feminine which is based on human instinct, unintegrated parts and unmet needs.

Healthy polarity is created when both people have healthy relationships with themselves first and then they play with consciously polarising their energies. This creates attraction in their relationships which comes from the heart.

I will explain this in clearer detail and examples later in the book, but this is where I find tantric practices and Tantra workshops very helpful because they help you to explore this healthy polarity within safe containers. This is also the foundation of what I teach in my tantric workshops and retreats.

David Deida has written some powerful books on masculine and feminine. I recommend checking out his work. I have referenced these in the back of the book, along with the ISTA website where you can find out about their trainings.

> **#LOVEDOWNLOAD: THE POLARITY CIRCLE**
>
> To help you with the next exercise I would like to give you access to my Polarity Circle PDF that I only usually give out at my workshops. The polarity circle shows you very clearly the qualities of each energy and how they interplay. You will also get access to a one-hour training video that goes much deeper into understanding the circle and how the behaviours, qualities, and polarities play out within relationships.
>
> Go to www.ejlove.com/polaritydload and you will be given immediate access to the PDF and video training.

Polarity Journalling Exercise:

What are the main traits and behaviours of the immature masculine that you have been in that need the most work on evolving?

_____
_____
_____
_____
_____
_____
_____

What are the main traits and behaviours of the wounded feminine that you have been in that need the most work on evolving?

_____
_____
_____
_____
_____
_____
_____

What qualities of the mature masculine do you see that you have that you can celebrate?

_____
_____
_____
_____
_____
_____
_____
_____
_____
_____

What qualities of the healthy feminine do you see that you have that you can celebrate?

_____
_____
_____
_____
_____
_____
_____
_____
_____
_____

Chapter 4

Embracing the Victimised Perspective

"True empowerment begins by allowing yourself to consciously experience and express the deep feelings of victimisation"

So let's start with the first step to healing your wounds. This is where you will actually go into fully feeling the victimisation of your past experiences.

You may be wondering why this is called "embracing the victimised perspective"; I mean, why would anyone want to be a victim of their experience?

Isn't this book about reclaiming our power?

Yes, it is!

But the reason for this is, that before we can come into a place of empowerment we have to allow ourselves to feel all the pain of what it felt like to be the victim in these experiences. What you are going to do in this chapter is really dive deep into all the resentments, frustrations, and complaints that you have or have had about a particular person or situation or men or women as a collective.

Calling Yourself Forward On Your Heart Protection Strategies

Although I very much agree that it is not healthy to be a victim of your past, there is a very specific way that the empowerment needs to happen, and it is NOT from pretending to be all tough and strong and just "moving on" as many people do. So I am here to lovingly call you forward on any heart protection strategies that you have disguised as empowerment!

There are two main ways to reclaim your power:
1. Vulnerability
2. Self-responsibility

The vulnerability of the healthy feminine and the self-responsibility of the mature masculine keeps you in your integrity, which keeps you living inside your values, and "ta da," this is what makes you live a happy, fulfilling life!

But you have to be willing to feel the pain, own your shit, and sometimes you are going to have to put your big-girl panties on (or grow some energetic balls) and have those vulnerable conversations about it!

If you avoid, withdraw, pull away, resist, over-boundary, numb, defend, deny, or diminish, then you ultimately are shutting down your heart to protect yourself. But this way will never lead to true empowerment.

As soon as you are trying to be powerful around someone or something from a place of fear, then you will be acting from a place of disempowerment and you will act out in ways that come from your ego.

Embracing the Victimised Perspective

> **#LOVEBOMB: YOUR EGO IS NOT BAD**
>
> Your ego is not wrong; ego has a purpose and its purpose is to help you survive and protect you from dying! According to Matt Kahn the ego is a sign of an over-stimulated nervous system. This sometimes serves you, but most of the time it does not. This is why clearing suppressed emotions will expand your consciousness and help you to be more heart-centred.

Have You Built a "Fuck-Off" Wall Around Your Heart?

Protecting yourself may help you in the moment, but it will never, ever serve you long term as you will be building a giant, energetic "fuck off" wall around your heart that is stopping you from attracting the kind of relationship that does serve you.

So you have to really be willing to let go of all the ways that you protect yourself and keep youself safe and then have the courage to be vulnerable!

If you look at me and see me as a powerful woman it is not because of what I do, it is because of how I show up so fully in my willingness to be self-responsible, in owning my "human as fuck" shit and then being willing to be vulnerable about it.

However, this is not to say that I am in my power all the time. One of the ways I disempower myself is when I am trying to prove myself or be "right" about things. Sometimes I still have to catch myself going into coaching people who haven't asked for my advice. This is the "fix it" jackal at its best!

This is one I have found hard to crack because it is part of the rescuer role that I developed from childhood that makes me feel safe and worthy. However, I am constantly exploring the way I show up in this and I am willing to be called on it!

Are You Willing To Be Called Forward On Your Shit?

My question to you is, are you willing to drop the masks and allow what's underneath that to be seen? If not, then you better stop reading this book now.

If YES, then let's dive into the questions below.

I want you to ask yourself the following questions and answer them in a journal or in the notes section at the back of this book. This will also lead into the work you will do in chapter 18 where you will reclaim your power from all the ways you have given it away.

- What am I most deeply afraid of?
- What makes me feel the most vulnerable?
- Where am I still protecting myself and my heart?
- What do I resist the most?
- What am I really avoiding here?
- How do I try to prove myself to others?
- How do I try to get love in unhealthy ways?
- What is it really costing me to show up this way?

Bypassing the Victimisation to Appear Strong

In our society, and particularly in spiritual and some personal development circles, I see that there has become this wrongness if you play the victim. I want you to notice if you are judging someone for this behaviour, because if you are then you are judging and suppressing the victim in yourself.

What I also mean by this is if you are unwilling to own and feel what it feels like to be the victim, then you may be bypassing that past pain and anger.

This was how I had been most of my life, having always been such a "strong independent woman" and hardly ever getting angry, and definitely not in front of other people!

"You are such a strong woman, EJ, after all you have been through," I would often get told.

I took this as a compliment because I thought this meant I was empowered, but no, what it really meant was that I was numbing my pain to avoid appearing weak. I wanted to be the cool, easygoing person that everyone liked. I needed to appear like I always had my shit together! What I didn't know was how much trying to be liked in this way was costing me and my happiness.

When Mindset Work Becomes an Emotional Bypass

I have worked with clients who are some of the top mindset coaches and entrepreneurs in the world. They have come to see me because even though they are super successful in business and awesome at manifesting their goals, they have a "fuck off" wall around their hearts. Often they are up in their heads trying to mindset everything, but the heart cannot be opened that way!

If shit came up for them, it was like "I'll just mindset that" or "I'll just journal on that so I can change how I feel about it."

But the emotions are held in the body, and this is where they must be felt and healed from. If you are not accessing and feeling your triggered emotions before doing mindset work then you could be using it as a form of emotional bypass.

One of the most common questions I ask my clients is, "How often do you get angry?"

They usually reply something like, "Hardly ever, I am not an angry person."

Yet, they have often been in unhealthy relationships where they have shut down feeling their full range of emotions and ended up in their heads. This was the way they had protected themselves, to freeze up or walk away whenever they felt afraid, and then go and focus on their careers or work as a form of avoidance.

Underneath that avoidance is the wild animal that has been long suppressed; and now it is time to unleash them!

I often say to them, "Well, it's time to get you angry!"

This is when I get my clients to do the next few exercises I am about to give you. This begins with a real willingness to access your victim story and tap into your wildness. This is when you will be able to fully feel and release the emotions that are sitting frozen in your body.

Shifting your mindset is still very important and this is why mindset coaches are so valuable. I even teach mindset myself and we will be doing mindset work in chapter 19. But that's a long way off so we have a bit of work to do before even getting to that!

You Must Have a Real Willingness to Heal

The very first step before stepping into healing yourself is having the WILLINGNESS to heal and I mean you have to be willing to release the identity that you have created to protect yourself.

Some people have so deeply engrained their identity from their past trauma, that they actually don't know who they are without it. For them, healing themselves is so incredibly scary and hence they may completely avoid and resist it.

This is why a gentle loving, compassionate approach to healing is what many people need, rather than trying to take someone into a big healing process to try and heal all their deep traumas overnight! That can be way too full on too fast and they can then be re-traumatised or snapback if the nervous system isn't ready for it. It will take longer going slow obviously, but the results are more permanent.

So, my point is that although you may want to heal all your shit super fast, your nervous system may not be ready for that and it would be a disservice if I promised you overnight healing! This is why we are taking things slowly in this book and why I designed these tools to be used over and over again, because everyday you get to use them and heal the nervous system at the level it is ready for. Then one day you notice that you don't show up the same way that you used to or the same shit just doesn't trigger you.

So I need two things from you here:-
1. To have a real willingness to heal
2. To be patient and trust the process

Can you do that?

Great! Let's get stuck into it…

What you are going to do over the next two chapters is access and feel the pain of being the victim of an experience, but you are not going to stay there!

After that we will completely pull the story apart and change the story into one of empowerment where you will create a new way of being in relationships.

Imagine a Time When You Were Triggered

I want you to now imagine a time when something triggered you and initially you felt frustrated and then you used your mind to try and understand it. You were trying to make sense of why it happened and perhaps you went into overanalysing it and you were all up in your head getting stressed out about it, playing the story over and over in your mind.

Underneath all of that heady stuff, the big piece you missed was actually allowing yourself to feel the frustration, anger, rage, and even deep grief that is most likely hiding underneath that trigger.

Your trigger is here to show you that there is pain there that is needing to be felt; this is where the treasure in the trigger is!

I secretly love it when I get triggered, because I know that it is such a huge opportunity to heal my wounds and deepen my self-love; even though it feels kinda shitty at the time, I know the bliss that is on the other side of it!

I know that it's never really about the other person, it's always about me learning how to love and feel myself more.

We are going to dive into understanding and managing your triggers in chapter six where I will give you some incredible tools to help you manage them and feel deep self-love.

The Victim as an Unhealthy Power

On the flip side of all of the above is when someone uses victimhood as a form of unhealthy power and protection. This usually would have started as a child, where the child got hurt and then they were given love and attention. They formed being the victim as part of their identity; this was their way of surviving and getting the love and approval they needed to feel safe.

So this is where people use their victimhood and their "poor me" stories to have people feel sorry for them, to get attention, to get love, to get their needs met. This has been most of my ex-partners!

This is why when I got to be the rescuer and they got to be the victim, there was so much attraction. We got to keep living out these survival patterns with each other. By understanding that playing the victim was their way of survival has also helped me to be more compassionate, whilst setting boundaries that I am not willing to engage with that behaviour.

Embracing the Victimised Perspective

So this is why even though you are about to go into the victimised perspective, you are not staying there! This is very, very important. You are NOT to stay there, so you have to promise me and yourself that you will read the chapters and do the exercises after this one, otherwise you might as well stop reading now and don't even do this exercise!

And if you choose not to go on, ask yourself "what am I really avoiding here and what is that costing me?"

And how long do you want to keep costing yourself all of that?

#LOVEPRACTICE: YOUR VICTIMISED STORIES

Whether you have bypassed being a victim or been an unhealthy victim to protect yourself, or flitted between the two, it's probably going to feel a bit shitty when you write this out from the victimised perspective. Especially if you are really good at mindset work and taking self-responsibility, you may want to say things like "he was lying to me, but I know it was because he was just trying to protect me" or "they really didn't mean to, it wasn't that bad" or "they were obviously just my mirror".

Hold your horses, I promise we are getting to that part!

I just need you to trust this process as mentioned above, okay? This process may take a little longer than you would like and you are going to have to feel some more shit than you may want to, but long term it's going to save you from even greater heartache.

Your future you will thank you big time!!

So this part is not about justifying or making sense of the person's behaviour. This is all about you getting to be upset about the way they treated and hurt you, no matter what the reason was for it.

I give you FULL PERMISSION to go "THERE" and go all loco crazy rage monster about it!

I want you to start by choosing just one relationship to focus on in this book. I want you to write out in bullet points below the biggest complaints, resentments, and frustrations that you have about the person and the relationship. If there are more relationships you need to heal, then you can re-do this process again and it gets faster and easier each time. Choose a more recent experience or preferably the most emotionally charged one from your adult life. We will be linking this up with your childhood later.

I want you to share below as though you are venting out all the things that person did to you or the ways that they hurt you, even if it was unintentional. Write it out as though no one is going to read it. This is just for you.

Let it all out, let it completely rip! No holding back! Trust the process!

For example:

- They hardly ever appreciated all the things I did for them
- I could not trust him to tell the truth
- They never took responsibility for anything, it was always on me
- She constantly lied to me and made up stories
- They cheated on me
- He was narcissistic and controlling
- They were emotionally and physically abusive
- He was never there for me
- I never felt supported by him
- No matter what I did it was never enough for them

Feeling All the Feels

Writing from a vicitimised perspective also may bring up emotions that may still be sitting there for you. It is VERY important to allow yourself to feel whatever comes up, cry to release the sadness and punch

Embracing the Victimised Perspective

pillows to release anger, reach out to the Facebook support group, or call a friend if you need to for support and to be heard.

Now it's your time to get it all out, so go ahead and write out the biggest complaints, resentments, and frustrations that you have about the person and/or relationship:

Chapter 5
Consciously Losing Your Shit

"Completely losing your shit is going to make you really happy!!"

It's time for you to let all that shit go!

Yes, you can now let go of the constant need to have it all together!

I give you full permission to let go of having to be the "good girl" or the "nice guy".

What sort of bullshit conditioning is that, really? I say—fuck that!

I want you to completely fuck off having to be the good girl or the nice guy.

I want you to let go of having to show up as the person who has it all together most of the time!

I want you to know how epically human you are and I want you to know that not one person on this planet "has their shit together," whatever that means!

Who the hell decided that you needed to be perfect anyway?

So give it up. Right here. Right now. Give it the fuck up.

Give that impossible standard of perfection up!

Because, by the way, I see you.

I see that you are not perfect and that you never will be, so what the hell are you trying to prove?

And who are you proving it to?

I Know What Happens Behind Closed Doors

I know that you get triggered as fuck sometimes and I know that you have vices and coping mechanisms that you don't want people to know about.

And then you put on a brave face to the world, pretending that everything is just fine.

People ask how you are and you say "I'm good" or "I've just been so busy."

When what you really want to do is scream and say "I've got so much going on right now, I don't how to handle it all, but I don't know how to ask for help because why would people want to help me? That's too much to ask, I'll look weak and I've been putting on this brave face for so damn long. I am scared to be truly vulnerable and open up, because I think people won't like me if they see the real me."

"I am the one that usually helps people! I can't show anyone that I don't want to do all of this on my own because the only way that people will love me and see me being of value is if I keep proving how good I am at having my shit together."

Yep. I told you—I see you.

Because I am you. This was me and sometimes it still is me. But I call myself on it now and I find it much easier to ask for help than I ever have before!

Stop Supressing your Wild Self-Expression

This is part of the good-girl syndrome or the nice-guy mask; you know, the old "children should be seen and not heard." This one I often heard my grandma say! For most people our childhood conditioning says it's not acceptable and and not safe to express all of ourselves and our emotions, especially for women to express anger and more commonly for men to express sadness.

Our full expression has been so shut down due to the parts of us that weren't accepted growing up having been suppressed. Human beings don't want to be seen as bad or weak, because we want to be liked so that we belong.

When we feel belonging, we feel safe. When we don't feel like we belong, we can feel a sense of abandonment and then that doesn't feel safe. We are always trying to keep ourselves safe and unconsciously run behaviours based on what we were taught growing up was 'acceptable' behaviour, this then completely runs our lives and relationships and most of the time we don't even know it!

So this is now your time to reclaim your expression from all the ways it has been shut down and deemed 'unacceptable' so that you have full permission to be the fullest most juiciest version of you!!

When I was at my first retreat in Bali I watched Brené Brown's TED Talk on the Power of Vulnerability. That was a massive lightbulb moment for me as I realised I had been numbing my whole life!

If you haven't watched this talk, I highly recommend you watch it again and again. It was a complete game-changer for me!

> ### #LOVEBOMB: HAPPINESS REQUIRES FEELING PAIN
>
> What stood out for me in Brené's talk was that she spoke to how we don't get a choice as to what emotions we numb. So when we suppress and shut down the expression of our uncomfortable emotions like anger and sadness, we also suppress feeling our happiness. This means to access inner joy, we actually have to be willing to feel our pain.

Losing Your Shit = Happiness

Now are you starting to see why I got you to go into the victimised perspective first?

To get you to start accessing your big pain points and the next piece to this is to really feel it in your body and release it in a healthy way. This will also prevent unhealthy outbursts and projecting onto others from a build-up of emotional suppression.

Long term it will also heal addictions and coping mechanisms that have only been serving to avoid feeling that pain. Ultimately it's going to help you feel a whole lot more of yourself, without making any of your emotional expression bad or wrong.

I want you to learn how to love the parts of you that feel anger, frustration, and sadness and embrace these parts as being what makes you an epic human being!

Over time the more you do the emotional release work the less pain there will be and the more joy you will feel. You see, happiness doesn't come from outside experiences, it comes from inside of you.

The Pot of Gold Doesn't Exist

Most people are trying to find happiness in moments and experiences rather than an inner-peace kind of happiness. If you are constantly searching for happiness in your life in anything outside of you, then you are wasting your time and energy and you will never get to that pot of gold at the end of the rainbow.

Because it doesn't exist.

Real happiness does not exist outside of you. Sure, things might make you feel happier, but you shouldn't be relying on these things to make you happy in the beginning.

Consciously Losing Your Shit

Like, let's say another person or a relationship. You should never choose to be in a relationship with a person because they make you feel better about yourself or because you were unhappy being alone.

It has to start from within and this comes from allowing yourself to feel your full range of emotions and filling yourself up with your own love first. Then, and only then, will you feel that spark of joy inside of your own heart that will radiate out into the rest of your life.

So how can you ever feel real joy inside of you, when you are shutting down your full emotional expression?

Yes, I'm basically saying that completely losing your shit is going to make you really happy!!

Consciously, of course; you are going to lose your shit in the most conscious way possible and sometimes you are not going to do it consciously because you are triggered as fuck and you can't be assed being conscious about it because your brain has gone into survival mode.

And that's when you are going to choose to love yourself even more.

Because that's what epic humans do.

They choose to love themselves more even when they are being unconscious and when they do that they heal their nervous system so that the next time it happens they can more easily make a more conscious choice. So the more you own and practice consciously losing your shit, the less you end up losing your shit unconsciously!

Clearing Emotional Blocks Out of the Body

Your emotions are held in your body as blocks and boulders and emotional release work clears the emotional body through vibration and moving energy and this goes deep into your cells. This can also reset your nervous system where cellular memory of your trauma is stored.

Your body has its own wisdom and it is far beyond the mind. Emotional release and expression exercises stop you from stressing and spilling that out into your relationships. It gets it out of your nervous system, letting life flow through so you can be much more alive!

If you resist doing any of this, then this is where the most emotional freedom is!

> ### #LOVEBOMB: WHEN YOU FEEL RESISTANCE
>
> *"Whatever you resist the most is where your greatest freedom is!"*
>
> I first heard these words when I was doing a Dancing Eros course on accessing the archetype - the Wild Woman. She was definitely the archetype I had the most resistance, and hence was the medicine I needed to fuck off my good girl mask and gave me permission to express deep rage that I had suppressed for too damn long. Remember this quote when you go to do any of the exercises in this book, and engrain it in your brain for the rest of your life!

#LOVEPRACTICE: RECLAIMING YOUR WILDNESS

1. SET UP A SAFE SPACE

To do this next exercise consciously it is best to find somewhere private with something soft that you can use for your body. In your bedroom on your bed with a pillow would be best. If you have kids, family, or flatmates you live with, I suggest finding a time when they are not around or you can could be courageous and tell them what you are doing and why so they have a heads-up about it. You could even encourage them to join in and do it too if they are open to it!

The main thing is you have to be somewhere that you feel completely safe to let go, somewhere that you won't hold yourself back, somewhere that you can give yourself full permission to let loose!

You can also ask a friend or coach to hold space for you. This is often a session I will take my clients through, especially if they get stuck accessing this part of themselves or they want to be taken deeper as I intuitively know what is needing to be released and how to take them there.

2. WILD MUSIC

What really gets my wildness activated is playing some heavy metal music, pumping it up, and punching a pillow and yelling into it! I have an emotional release playlist you can follow on Spotify; the link to it is listed is in the resources section at the back of this book.

The music is to help you access those feelings with the intention of clearing the emotional blocks being held in your body.

3. FEELING AND RELEASING THE VICTIMISATION

You are going to focus on the relationship or person you wrote about in the last chapter. Read over the victimised perspective again and really feel into how you felt when that person did those things to you and how upsetting it was. You may feel this rising in your body. It is okay if it feels numb too, usually underneath numbness are a whole lot of feelings that have been trapped and suppressed for a long time!

You can even visualise this person sitting in front of you or visualise their head on a pillow as you punch it.

Trust how your body wants to move and make sure you are breathing, bringing in sound, which can be done in screaming or yelling, and even words; swear words are great! Think about all the things you wanted to say to that person that you never got to say. Now is the time to let all that crazy shit out!

You are to use movement such as jumping up and down, pillow punching and shaking your body!

4. GIVE YOURSELF FULL PERMISSION TO GO CRAZZZY

That's it— go get your wildness on!

Let it look however it needs to look: messy, ugly, animalistic… it's all welcome!

Act like a little kid and throw a big old temper tantrum … let that little (or big) rage monster out of its cage!

Connect to the child inside of you who got told not to cry or get angry, because now it is time to fully self-express all that you didn't get to back then. You don't have anyone now to tell you that it's not okay and this is where you will be liberated from all that emotional suppression!

This is your emotional freedom baby!!

If you think that if anyone saw you they would think you are a crazy person, then this is exactly what I want you to be doing!

Yes, I want you to look like a completely crazy person!

You may be doing this in the privacy of your own home, or if you prefer out in nature in a forest can be an even better way to release all your shit!

Spend AT LEAST five minutes doing this and if you want to keep going for longer, just go with it!

Sometimes I have done this for an hour and I find huge shifts happen after that. You will know when you feel complete. You can always come back to this again if you feel there is still more there towards this person to be released.

5. BE GENTLE ON YOURSELF

After you have done this spend at least 10 minutes resting to integrate the experience. Shift to a more gentle, chilled type of music. Be with any emotions that may have risen. Tears may rise at this stage, as often there is deep grief sitting underneath the anger.

If You Are Struggling, Freezing, Resisting, or Too in Your Head

If you find it hard to get started or you go into a numb or frozen state and are too up in your head then move into a foetal position if you can and then tense up your whole body really tightly whilst holding your breath. After you have held that for a little while let out the breath and rest the body. Do this until you start to feel the body wanting to move if it does. Don't try to force anything, take this very gently.

If you are able to, you can also start shaking your hands and fingers and build this up slowly until your whole body is able to shake.

Make sure that you are not going into the story of what happened. Often people telling the story in detail of what happened is coming from the head, not the body, and is another way to bypass feeling the painful emotions.

Instead of telling the story, keep asking 'how did that make you feel? and start shaking those hands, and even if you just do this every day for two weeks for a couple of minutes this will help you open your body. Then go and attempt to do the above exercise.

If you are resisting this practice or making excuses like "I don't have time right now," then this is where the gold is!

Your body has probably been waiting a very long time for you to feel all of this. Sometimes it can feel absolutely terrifying and unsafe to come back into your body. You can also ask someone to be there to guide and hold space for you. You can give them this book to guide and encourage you into the practice or do it together.

Whatever you find the most challenging is usually where the biggest growth is, so keep going; I promise it will be worth it!

#LOVEPRACTICE: COMMIT TO LOSING YOUR SHIT DAILY

For the next two weeks I want you to practise doing this for at least five minutes a day. You don't have to have a specific intention or release towards a person, unless you really feel you need to.

Anger is not a bad emotion, it is an emotion that needs to be fully seen, felt, loved, and released by ourselves. It is part of being human and the healing process, so it is time to embrace it and let it out in a healthy way!

If you make anger wrong, you shame yourself, which only leads to more numbness, disconnection, and a lack of self-love.

From now on, you are to commit to feeling your anger and consciously losing your shit for the rest of your life!

Every time you feel just a teensy bit of frustration or are in your head over-analysing, check in and ask yourself "what is really wanting to be felt here?" Then go get your wildness on!

You will really get to know if there is something sitting there to be released, because the more you do these practices the more you come back into your body and become in tune with its wisdom.

Eventually the more you consciously lose your shit, the less you will actually lose your shit, because you won't need to do this as much.

But every time you stop yourself from feeling frustration or anger you are creating disconnection and suppression in your emotional body. Not only does it suppress happiness, but if you don't feel it when it comes up, it will only get triggered again at a later time.

It is better to feel it to heal it when it comes up in the moment!

I want you to write this here or something that feels more aligned for you: "I give myself permission not to have all my shit together. I commit to consciously losing my shit regularly."

I GIVE MYSELF PERMISSION TO …

I COMMIT TO …

#LOVELIST: INVOKING DEEP FEELINGS

On the next pages is a list I created of ways that work for me to feel my emotions when they come up. It is important for me to take the time to be with myself and my feelings. Often when I feel even just a slight tinge of sadness come up I will go and put on a sad song and listen to it to fully feel that sadness.

Sometimes it wants to come up in tears and sometimes it doesn't. Sometimes I just need to put my hand on my heart and breathe in and acknowledge that I am feeling sad.

I use the wording "I am feeling sad" rather than "I am sad" to distinguish between myself and my feelings. Because we are not our feelings and the language we use is so important in identifying this. This way I am more in ownership of the feeling rather than it owning me!

Often I will ask myself "what do I need to fully feel this?" and I see what my body has to say. Sometimes it might just be sending love to the part of me that feels sad. It may be that I need to go for a walk or go to the beach and it may mean I have to say no to something else I had planned. It's about constantly making the choice to feel instead of numb. It is those simple choices in those small moments that add up to long-term happiness.

Every day you have this choice, so it's important to really start being an observer to what you do when you notice an uncomfortable feeling come up.

For example, if you notice a slight sadness or frustration come up, do you start scrolling social media, eat something, or call a friend to distract you? Do you have a drink or cigarette or binge on movies or TV? Watch porn and/or masturbate?' These are the ways we often disassociate from our feelings and lead to addictions.

It is those moments that you acknowledge and name your feelings and then ask yourself "What do I most need right now? What do I need to feel this?"

It is helpful to have a list of ways that invite in your feelings to refer to. You can use mine if you like and/or create your own on the following page. Write out what works for you when you feel bottled up too (that is NOT a coping mechanism).

Also, be willing to try something that isn't comfortable for you, that is not your 'go to'. If you find it easy to cry, ask yourself 'what am I really angry about?' and use the wildness practice. If you get angry easily, ask yourself 'what am I really sad about?' and then listen to some sad music and look into your own eyes in the mirror and tell yourself it's safe for you to feel sadness, mimic sad sounds and sniffles to help bring up the sadness more.

EJ's List of Ways to Invoke Deep Feelings

- **Consciously lose my shit** – Use the wildness reclamation practice to get any resentment, anger, and rage out. Allow the emotions to move through me.

- **Nurture my inner child** – Tell my inner child that I am here for her and that I love her and ask her what she needs. Go play outside, give myself a big hug. Think about how I would want to be comforted as a child and give myself that comfort.

- **Hugs** – Ask someone for a hug or a way in which I would like to be held.

- **Group circles and being heard** – Vulnerable sharing of my emotions and what is going on for me, hearing others share their vulnerabilities and stories.
- **Sharing my vulnerability** – Sharing my vulnerable feelings with friends and family. Asking for their permission to hear me first and asking them to hold space for me to be heard before offering me any advice.
- **Write a letter to the person** – However, I may not actually send it. Look at the intention behind why I want to send it as writing it may be enough. Stay connected to that individual. Don't rush it, keep writing it until I feel fully and truly self-expressed. If I decide to send it, do it only when I am coming from a healthy space, not a triggered space.
- **Being held space for** – Get a friend to hold space for me to rage out / cry / feel my emotions.
- **Nature** – Get into nature, go for a walk, and be present with my feelings
- **Time alone and journalling** – Spend time alone, just being with myself, journalling and writing everything out that is coming up for me.
- **Crying** – Crying and letting the tears come and not wiping them away immediately so that I detox more.
- **Mirror work** – Doing mirror work where I look deeply into my eyes and give myself words of comfort, love, and safety, such as "I love you, I am here for you, you are safe."
- **Music** – Listen to music that invites deep feeling. I can also do it in the car; go for a drive and just be with what comes up.
- **Exercise** – Dancing and/or yoga. Exercise such as boxing to release strong emotions.

Now it's your turn to write out your own list of ways to invoke deep feelings.

My List of Ways to Invoke Deep Feelings

Chapter 6

Emotional Triggers as a Pathway to Self-Love

"Triggers are gifts that have come to show you the wounds that are needing to be healed and loved."

Yep ... here we go ... let's talk about those freaking triggers ...

Oh boy, our relationships are always a surefire way to make sure all the emotions we suppress will be shown to us when someone triggers the fuck out of us!

This then gives us a huge opportunity to use these triggers as a pathway to deep healing and self-love, if we choose it. If we learn how to manage them, rather than project them onto the other person or run away from them or shut down!

Finding the Trigger in the Treasure

Emily Orum, one of my mentors, says that there is always a treasure in the trigger! There is a process to go through to discover this and that requires identifying that we are telling ourselves a story when we get triggered, feeling the emotions underneath that story, and then identifying the unmet needs that are sitting under all of that.

So a trigger is simply a sign of emotions that need to be expressed and needs that want to be met. Identifying these gives us the opportunity to feel the emotions and to meet our own needs, rather than expecting someone else to soothe our pain and meet our needs for us.

Managing and healing your triggers is actually a beautiful gift and creates an amazing opportunity to know and love yourself more deeply. In this chapter you are going to learn to understand your triggers and learn how to use them as a pathway for healing that ultimately deepens you into self-love and greater connection with yourself and others.

Most of the learnings in this chapter have come from or been inspired by the teachings of Scott Catamas from the Love Coach Academy and Emily Orum (the Heart Ninja). They have been incredible teachers of mine.

Although they have given me permission to share anything they have taught me, I really wanted to honour their work here. So please check out their websites listed in the resources section in the back of the book and make sure you follow them on social media. I will be forever grateful to these wonderful human beings, because if it wasn't for their wisdom, kindness, patience, support, and compassion during my time healing from abuse I don't know if I would be where I am today.

Managing Your Emotional Triggers

Before my relationship with Leo I had never really thought about managing my triggers. I didn't seem to have any big triggers when I was on my own and this is why it seemed like it was more about the other person than me!

In the past I would have used alcohol, cigarettes, or sex to simply numb my feelings when I was triggered.

However, I knew that we were triggering each other's deepest wounds. I knew that he was triggering all these parts of me that felt rejected, abandoned, unworthy, and not good enough, as it was also for him, because he was a mirror for all of them.

Whilst I was in this relationship I watched Scott Catamas speak on "Managing your Emotional Triggers"; it was EXACTLY what I needed to hear!

What I discovered from working with Scott and Emily was that even though we may want to blame the other person, we have to take responsibility for our own feelings and needs. If we don't learn how to manage and understand our emotional triggers it can ruin our relationships, our work, and any real possibility for joy and happiness as we can become so disconnected from ourselves and the people in our lives.

Please note though, there is no excuse for abusive behaviour and if someone is not willing to take personal responsibility for their emotions and triggers, then this is a sign of leading to an unhealthy relationship. My suggestion in this situation would be to take a look at what your dealbreakers and boundaries are for being in a relationship. We will talk more about this later on in the book too.

The Three F Words

Fight, Flight, and Freeze ... these are the three main reactions that we have when we get triggered (and sometimes all of them at different times). This happens when the reptilian part of your brain is perceiving that you are being attacked in some way as it thinks you are in physical survival still.

Fight is the reaction that presents as defending or attacking which can come out in words, body language, tone and volume of voice, which then tends to trigger the other person more.

Flight is when you want to run away from and ignore the situation or person and you don't want to deal with it or you don't know how to.

Freeze is when the body can completely freeze up and you become numb to what is going on and often can't even move or speak.

In any of these reactions there can also be a tendency to turn to numbing and avoidance behaviours such as smoking, alcohol, drugs, sex, working, keeping busy, or even something simple such as turning to social media and Facebook scrolling! This is a way to distract yourself and "check out" of having to feel the pain of what has been triggered.

I found that my survival reaction was fight in that relationship and then flight. I would fight and then walk off, then come back to have my say and then walk off and then come back and so on—back and forth, back and forth.

Until eventually I gave up and waited until I felt better and hoped the person was over it too and I could get my needs met … finally!

That was until the next time I got triggered!

And repeat …

Tend and Befriend

Tend and Befriend is another instinctual reaction that has more recently come into our awareness. According to Wikipedia "Tend-and-befriend is a behavior exhibited by some animals, including humans, in response to threat. It refers to protection of offspring (tending) and seeking out the social group for mutual defense (befriending). In evolutionary psychology, tend-and-befriend is theorized as having evolved as the typical female response to stress, just as the primary male response was fight-or-flight."

How Triggers Play Out in Your Relationships

We often project our past pain onto another person and blame them for making us feel a certain way or hurting us when often it has nothing to do with them at all. It is our past shit that is coming up to be seen, loved, and healed. Of course, the other person also tends to do the same thing to us! This can then lead to a vicious cycle of blame and building up a whole lot of resentment, especially if it doesn't ever get talked about in a conscious, connected way.

This is why I believe most couples end up separating: they never talk about what happens after a fight. They just wait until the storm is over and carry on with life like nothing happened. However the more this happens the more they trigger each other until they are fighting all the freaking time from having a build up of resentment.

You then have two people trying to function in a relationship with very low love tanks, unmet needs, and who are both giving their power away. They think they have fallen out of love, but usually the truth is that they put their attention on the relationship or on their busy lives and stopped meeting their own needs and values and filling their love tank first, and then blamed the other person for that. They also may have stopped communicating and being vulnerable about their feelings. Without vulnerability, you cannot have a deeply connected relationship.

When Your Triggering Triggers the Other Person

What I have often witnessed is someone who goes into fight mode with someone who goes into flight or freeze. Their triggers polarise each other and lead to even more triggering! You then have one person fighting, wanting to get the other person to react and talk, which only sends that other person more into flight or freeze.

If both people are in fight mode they are often trying to be right about their point of view. This used to happen with Leo; we would both end up talking over the top of each other until eventually it turned into yelling, both of us desperately wanting to be heard and thinking that somehow if one of us spoke louder then the other would listen!

Well, it never quite worked that way; you will never, ever sort a conflict out or be heard when both people are triggered. This is when it is important to take some time out for both of you to feel and process your feelings and then come back and talk about it when you are no longer triggered and can discuss from a clear and calm space.

Whilst in the reptilian brain nothing will make sense and people will say things they really don't mean and it will be one gigantic downward spiral if you keep reacting from this place.

What you need to be aware of is that when people are triggered they aren't really them; they are only the animal primal instinct part of them, not the heart-centred part of them. I try to never take anything personally when someone is triggered, because it's never about me, it's always about them trying to get their needs met, often from me.

> **#LOVETIP: HOLDING SPACE FOR ANOTHER'S TRIGGER**
>
> When someone is triggered and they want you to hold space for them, some powerful questions to ask from a place of curiosity are:
>
> "What do you need right now? How can I support you?"
>
> If you are listening to them share their point of view, you can say in a calm tone sentences such as:
>
> "I hear you, I get it, what else?"
>
> This will help diffuse the situation and may help the person to calm down and feel safe enough to share what is really going on for them.

Resolving Conflict and Coming Back into Connection

This process below is one that was inspired by Scott and Emily's teachings and I give it to people to use when they get triggered. This can also be given to both people to follow the process and then come back and share why they got triggered, what came up for them, what they can take responsibility for, and what they are needing from the other person.

Emotional Triggers as a Pathway to Self-Love

You can't expect the other person to meet your needs, but you can look at how you can meet your own needs and make agreements to support each other with that. This process can be used to resolve conflict with anyone that you get triggered by, not just in your romantic relationships.

Step 1: Stop and Breathe

As soon as you start to feel triggered—stop and breathe!

When you go into survival mode the brain thinks you are dying, so you actually often stop breathing. If you start to take deep breaths then you are telling the brain that yes, you are still alive!

I know it sounds crazy, because of course you know that you are still alive, but the reptilian brain does not and this is why you may stop breathing when you are triggered.

Taking slow, deep breaths in through the mouth and out through the nose (yes, I said that right). This will calm your nervous system.

The only time this may not work is when you are in freeze and can't breathe. This is when you go into holding the breath and tensing your body up as suggested in the last chapter.

It is also important to know how a trigger feels in your body. Most people feel sensations like heat, sweating, swelling, shaking, temperature rising, and tension in their body when they start to get triggered. If you can identify the sensations you feel in your body then you will know when you are going into a trigger and this is when you can remind yourself to start the breathing.

Step 2: Take a Time Out

If you are being triggered by someone and cannot have a calm conversation with them, then this is when you take a time out. Scott calls this a "connected time out," essentially you are reassuring each other that you are not running away or abandoning ship (which may trigger abandonment wounds), but that you are taking time out to process until you become calm enough to have a conscious conversation.

You could say to the person: "I am feeling triggered right now and I need to take some time out to feel this and I will come back and talk to you when I am calm".

Step 3: Ask Yourself—What Are the Stories I Am Telling Myself?

Write out everything that is going on in your head. Do a brain dump and get it all out!

All the complaints, all the wrongs and resentments, and everything you are blaming them for. So it will be things like "he doesn't care about me, she doesn't respect my feelings, it's not fair, I can never have what I want, I am rejected, they don't love me" and so on.

These are all the stories in your monkey mind that you are telling yourself over and over and over. You know the ones I mean, where you can't stop obsessing about something and you wish your head would shut the hell up already!

You can write them all out or if you can't do that in the moment then ask yourself the question "what are the stories I am telling myself?" and notice them in your mind from an observer's point of view.

You then say to yourself 'I can see that I am telling myself a story that (insert story)'

Step 4: Name and Embrace the Feelings

Underneath all those stories are all your uncomfortable emotions such as anger, sadness and disappointment.

This trigger is signalling to you that these emotions need to be felt, expressed and released.

Ask yourself—"What am I feeling here?"

Put one hand on your heart and say "I am feeling **insert emotion**" and breathe deeply into your heart.

Do this for each emotion.

Allow any other emotions to surface and for these to be expressed.

If tears start to flow then be with them and allow them to fall rather than wiping them away immediately.

If anger or frustration is coming up then express and release them via pillow punching, screaming, shaking your body, and so on.

Often if my emotions are really charged, I will skip identifying the stories and just go straight to feeling the emotions. However, I have the awareness that it is a story from past pain that is triggering this.

Step 5: Identify Your Needs

Underneath your uncomfortable emotions are your unmet needs.

So, for example, the main emotions I had when I got triggered with Leo were sadness, disappointment, upset, frustration, anger, and fear.

What I needed was to be heard, to be understood, respect, empathy, compassion, intimacy, and physical touch.

Back then I didn't have this process and I didn't understand what was going on, but if I did I would have been able to handle the situation a lot differently!

Step 6: Meet Your Needs

Now here is the opportunity to learn how to self-source and meet your own needs, rather than expecting the other person who triggered you to do this for you.

Ask yourself—"How can I meet these needs?"

It might be things like going for a walk, self-nurture, positive self-talk, talking to a friend, meditation, self-compassion and self-empathy practices, physical touch with self, or asking for a hug from someone else.

If you don't know how to give self-compassion or self-empathy right now, I'll be taking you through a self-soothing inner-child mirror-work exercise further in this chapter.

Because it is really just the *little you* that has been triggered. Your inner child that is hurt and isn't feeling safe. When you self-soothe you are being the adult, giving yourself the love and attention that you didn't get met as a child in these moments.

Step 7: Have the Conscious Conversation

If it was someone that triggered you and you need to clear it with them then have the conversation about it. It doesn't matter if they have done this process too or not. Ideally if you are in a romantic relationship it would be powerful if you both read this chapter and committed to practicing this when you both get triggered.

Ultimately though, it's about you sharing your truth. I have found that when I take ownership of my feelings and needs it inspires the other person to do the same. I don't expect them to, but I also have boundaries around not connecting intimately with people who aren't willing to also be self-responsible. This has helped me to curb my tendency to be overly responsible also!

You may not even need to talk to the person though. Perhaps that person triggered you and it hasn't actually affected your relationship, and you know that it is something you simply needed to look at within yourself. Sometimes our triggers can also be inspiring - where we see something in someone else that we want more of in ourselves. The more conscious we are about our triggers that more grateful we become for them.

Incredible healing happens when we bring our triggers into the light and discuss them openly with one another. This is where the real magic and connection happens, when we own and show people the not so shiny and nice parts of ourselves!

When you have the conversation the best way is to share the most important parts of what you have just processed above. Make sure to come from a place of full self-responsibility rather than blame.

Here is a template:-

"When you did/said XYZ, I made it mean that / I told myself that (enter stories you were telling yourself here) which brought up feelings of (enter emotions here). I realised that what I am really needing is (enter needs here)."

You may also like to share a time where you felt this way before; perhaps it was a childhood experience that was triggered. Then the other person can ideally drop into your reality and see that it was from a past wound and wasn't even really about them (especially if they have taken it personally).

Step 8: Ask for Support

You can then share whether you have found a way to meet your needs or ask them if they are willing to help you.

You ask, "Are you able to support me / help me meet these needs?"

You have to be willing to hear no, otherwise it becomes a demand and not a request.

If they say no, then you could ask, "Is there anything you need from me to be able to help meet these needs?"

For example sometimes it might be that they cannot help you right now, but if you gave them some more time then they could help you when they are available. There may also be a fear in their space that may be preventing them from saying yes. Make it clear that you are not trying to change their boundary, but are curious if there might be anything they too are needing.

Again, you have to be willing to hear no. The last thing you want them to do is to give their power away and agree to do something they don't want to, as this will build more resentment and more conflict and triggering down the track.

If they say no then say, "Thank you for honouring yourself," and then find a way to meet your own needs or self-soothe or ask someone else for support. You simply can't rely on one person to meet your needs, so it is important to have a good outside support network who can also help you meet them.

If they say yes, this is when you can create agreements to meet these needs in a way that feels good for both of you.

It may even be as simple as a hug!

Give them an opportunity to also share with you what came up for them. You must also be willing to hear their side, their stories, their feelings, and their needs and see if you can be willing to help meet their needs (without crossing your own boundaries).

When they are sharing, don't interrupt them or try to defend yourself. Be in curiosity and hear them out and you can also use the words "I hear you, I get it, is there anything else?"

Once you have both shared, you can make new agreements to support each other to meet your own needs and meet the needs of the other that you are willing and able to meet.

I always find it's nice to end with checking in to see that you both feel complete and have some physical touch such as a hug, but make sure you check in with the person first to ask if they are open to receiving it.

Trigger Healing and Conscious Conversation Example:

If I go back in time to when I was lying in bed feeling triggered and frustrated because I wanted to get cuddles but armed with the knowledge that I have now, this is what I would have done differently:

I would have taken myself through the process of asking myself what stories am I telling myself? What am I feeling? What am I needing?

I then would have asked him if he was willing to have a conversation about what is alive in me (and be prepared to hear no).

I would have said:

"When you said you didn't want to come and cuddle me in bed, I made it mean that you don't care about me and I told myself that I am not important to you. This brought up feelings of disappointment and sadness. Underneath this I realised that what I am really needing is to be held and have intimacy and physical touch with you, this helps me feel really loved. Is there a way that you could help me meet these needs?"

Now, if Leo was a healthy man, I am imagining that he may have expressed that he wanted to get his needs met for time on his own where he could just zone out by watching movies. I imagine that a good agreement which could have been made is that three or four nights a week he could have watched movies and the other nights I could have got my cuddle time with him.

I want to make an important point here though that this would most likely not have worked with Leo because he was not a healthy man. Leo deliberately did not give me cuddles because he knew it triggered me, this was his way of getting narcissistic supply.

What I found interesting was though as soon as I let go of the idea of getting cuddles from him and stopped getting triggered by it, he started coming to bed again and then he wanted to spend every night cuddling me!

I am not saying to use this tool as a way to get a narcissist to try and stop triggering you! Because depending where they are on the narcissist spectrum, they may find other ways to trigger you. I'll be talking about the narcissistic spectrum later in the book.

When using this with another person, for it to work they need to be healthy and willing to listen to you and able take responsibility for their part too. Ultimately this is not even about the other person, it's about you learning about your triggers and having this conversation with people who are willing to hear you, lean into vulnerability and evolve your relationship.

If you are unsure about whether someone in your life is a narcissist, in chapters 9 and 13 I will be explaining narcissism in greater detail.

Whether someone is healthy or not, this is about you doing it for you most of all!

LOVE PRACTICE: THE TRIGGER HEALING PROCESS

Think about a time when someone triggered you recently. How did you react?

_____
_____
_____

What stories did you tell yourself?

_____
_____
_____

What were you feeling?

_____
_____
_____

Emotional Triggers as a Pathway to Self-Love

What were you needing?
_____
_____

What can you see that you could have done differently now?
_____
_____

What conversation would you have had?
_____
_____

Is there a conversation like this that you need to have with someone? Who?
_____
_____

Write out the words below and then ask to have that conversation:
_____
_____
_____

Not Shaming the Triggers

The important thing to remember is that getting triggered is not bad or wrong. See your triggers as gifts that have come to show you what wounds are next to be healed and to be loved. This is a huge opportunity for healing and growth, if you choose to see them this way.

It's about taking a step back and looking at them as an observer, going gently on yourself, and practising self-empathy and self-compassion.

It is also important not to judge yourself or the other person when they get angry and reactive.

Don't say things like "you are just triggered" or "you are such an angry person."

Saying this will likely fuel it and make it worse.

> **#LOVETIP: RESPONDING TO SOMEONE WHO IS TRIGGERED**
>
> In the book *Communication Miracles for Couples* by Jonathan Robinson, he suggests using the following words to respond to someone who is triggered.
>
> "It sounds like (fill in using their words) that must feel … (fill in the emotion), I'm really sorry that feels that way for you." Then you can ask, "What do you need from me?"
>
> This then gives them an opportunity to express their underlying need. By using these words the person will generally feel like they are being heard, that you are acknowledging their reality, and validating their feelings and their experience.

You Have a Right to Feel What You Feel

When someone says "well, you shouldn't feel that way," then it is invalidating someone's feelings and that person's reality in that moment. Even though the trigger is from a past wound, it feels incredibly real for the person and the feelings are definitely real.

Give Your Triggers a Voice

Make a conscious effort to learn about your triggers and the triggers of the people closest to you.

In the below exercise write a list of all the things that trigger you and make you feel the most vulnerable. This will also help you identify what your deepest wounds and pain points are, which will be helpful as you continue to read and dive into the rest of this book.

For example, my biggest triggers in the past have been around being ignored, feeling as though someone has withdrawn their love in some way, feeling unwanted and rejected, abandoned, not being communicated with openly, not feeling chosen, other women, feeling deceived and betrayed, being lied to, feeling like I'm missing out on something and not being included, feeling like my time is being wasted or disrespected, feeling let down by others.

It can also be certain words, phrases, tone of voice or body language that can trigger us easily. For example, if someone comes right up into someone's personal space it could be a trigger for them. Whereas for someone else it may not trigger them at all.

You can then take this list and share it with your loved ones and you can get them to do the same. This helps you to be more compassionate towards one another, as we all have different triggers. Whilst remembering that you are not responsible for someone else's trigger.

It's learning about each other's differences and honouring these rather than making them wrong. These are the areas where you also need to go gently on yourself!

#LOVEPRACTICE: IDENTIFYING YOUR TRIGGERS

What are the things that trigger you? Write out a list below.

_____
_____
_____
_____
_____
_____
_____
_____
_____

Are than any specific words, phrases, tone of voice, or body language that triggers you?

_____
_____
_____
_____
_____
_____
_____
_____
_____

Making This a Daily Practice

I don't get triggered so much by what I shared above these days; this is because I have been practising the trigger-healing process constantly. I have made it a habit and it is what has become familiar for my brain now. I have moved more out of survival brain and more into the frontal lobe whilst healing the nervous system—yay!

Of course I am still human and I still have a reptilian brain so I still get triggered, I just tend to manage this differently now. Rather than fighting someone, I will take some deep breaths first and then check in with myself as to what is coming up for me.

I may have to take some space from a person I am triggered by, but I don't see this as running away. I see this as taking the time I need to process and feel my emotions and to look into what this is really about, to hold space for myself. Ultimately I know it's not about them, it's about me. I reassure them of that by telling them that this is what I am doing.

One time I said to a lover, "I am feeling really triggered right now, I need some time to process what I am feeling, but I am committed to working through this. Even though my brain is in survival, my heart and soul is committed to staying connected to you."

His response was, "I feel that too, thank you, that feels good in my heart."

We then made a commitment to talk again when we both had enough space to process what had happened. From that space we would then come back into connection and share from clarity rather than from story and projecting blame.

Remembering to Do These Practices

Like any new habit, it took some time to remember do this process each time I got triggered. It is the hardest thing to remember to do anything logically and consciously when you are triggered!

So I don't always get this perfect, but I am compassionate on myself for how I show up and I will always, always own my part in it with the other person. My integrity is in having the vulnerable conversations to resolve the conflict and come back into connection if the other person is willing to do so.

When your inner child is triggered, this is when you need to call on your inner parent to hold space for yourself, take deep breaths, and empower yourself to use the trigger healing process.

A good example of how I have used my triggers to feel anger was when I was an escort and I sometimes had clients who would just not show up. I would get so shitty and frustrated because I felt they were wasting my time (I called these men "fucking timewasters"). I would then do the trigger healing process and use this as an opportunity to feel suppressed anger and resentment I had towards men!

When I asked myself who I was really angry at, I found that I was really angry at myself for all the ways I had been wasting my own time!

Eventually I stopped getting triggered by them and all my clients started showing up for me more than ever because I didn't run that story as being real and true anymore.

#LOVEGIFT: THE TRIGGER HEALING PROCESS

I have put this emotional trigger process into an easy-to-follow, one page, step-by-step healing process to go to as soon as you find yourself being triggered. This is a downloadable file that you can get immediate access to at www.ejlove.com/triggerprocess.

Once you have downloaded it take a snapshot of it on your phone and make sure to save it to your favourites so you can find it easily—it will be your saviour!

You can also print it out and have it somewhere close by where you can refer to it until it becomes a habit. You will also get access to a video on how to use this process.

If there is only one practice you take away and really embody from this book, please let it be this one!

Soothing the Inner Child With Self-Empathy

One of the most powerful practices when you feel triggered is to show up as your own parent, particularly if you can't or don't know how to meet your own needs.

When you do this you are talking to your inner child, your little girl or boy who is hurting, and you give them the words and touch that helps them feel safe and loved that they perhaps didn't get as a child.

#LOVEPRACTICE: Inner Child Mirror Work

Look into your wall mirror or use a hand mirror.

If you don't know how to meet your own needs you can say:

"Hi little (your name), I don't know how to meet your needs right now, but I just want you to know that I am here for you. I love you."

You can keep repeating words such as "I am here for you, you are safe, I love you, please forgive me. I didn't mean to hurt you. It's not your fault. I know you are doing the best that you can."

If you feel disconnected from your inner child, simply speak to that and say what's really there, such as 'I am finding it hard to connect to you, but I am leaning into and learning how to be here for you now.'

Your relationship with your inner child is vital to having healthy relationships. If your abandon your little one and their needs, then you are withdrawing love from yourself and this will generally get reflected back in how you are treated by another. Unfortunately this kind of inner relating has not been modelled to us as children and has even been deemed as 'selfish'. In my experience taking care of my inner child has to be a priority - without having her fully included and on board nothing works. There is no way I can relate in healthy ways with others. She is the most important relationship I will ever have and has to come before any relationship outside of myself.

I highly recommend to have a daily practice to cultivate this relationship where you tune in with your inner child, check in and acknowledge them and see if they have any needs they need met by your adult self.

You may find that your inner child has been waiting a very long time to be met, seen and fully acknowledged by you!

This practice is simple yet extremely powerful.

Chapter 7

The "Twin Flame" Spiritual Awakening

"Every time you are seeking love outside of yourself, you are abandoning the love that you are"

Have you experienced a "twin flame" connection? Or perhaps a super intense soulmate connection that you were so very sure that this person was "*the one*"?

But you couldn't understand why they kept running away or saying things to you but their actions were never quite aligning … or they kept triggering the fuck out of you and no matter how much you tried, you just couldn't seem to make the relationship work!

It became co-dependent and maybe even toxic.

Meet what I call the "woundmate" or what some people may refer to as a false twin flame or karmic soulmate.

I put the word "twin flame" in inverted commas because I know that this was not a true twin flame connection for me as I once believed it was. Through working with my love coaching clients, I discovered that so many others have been through a similar "twin flame" spiritual awakening experience.

My Twin Flame Story Went a Little Something Like This ...

In 2012 I met Charlie.

When I first met him I was unsure as to whether I was all that attracted to him, but after he charmed the pants off me (literally!) and talking for hours and telling me that "I was just so fascinating," I started to really like him, especially when one day he just disappeared off the face of the earth!

This left me in complete devastation, confusion, and questioning everything about myself and going over things trying to find out what I must have done wrong. Because surely, I thought, there must have been something wrong with me!

A week later he eventually resurfaced telling me that he got scared and that he wasn't ready for the intensity of our connection, but that he still wanted to try with me and take things slow.

But slow to him meant showing me hardly any interest at all.

He had gone from being super interested in me, as though I was the most amazing woman he had ever met and telling me that he had never felt this kind of connection before, telling his friend that I was "the one", to being really distant and saying things like "I don't want to hurt you."

This brought all my deepest wounds—rejection, abandonment, and not feeling good enough.

My initial reaction to feeling this deep pain was by completely stuffing my face with food—chocolate, lollies, ice cream, and chips—making myself so full that I felt sick.

I would then purge.

I Had Bulimia for 10 Years

I had by this time suffered from bulimia on and off for 10 years. I had never really considered that it was a big problem because I told myself that "it wasn't all the time." Sometimes I would go months without purging, other times it would be every meal, every day for weeks.

But by this time I had finally admitted to myself that I needed to get some help because I didn't want to be years down the track and still struggling with this. I knew it wasn't normal or healthy for me and one day I wanted to be able to have children and I knew if I kept going I may have completely ruined my chances for that.

I was scared to ask for support though, and more so I felt so ashamed by it. I was ashamed that I even had an eating disorder and even more ashamed that I had hidden it for so long from my friends and family. It was the shame that was also keeping me stuck in the cycle of the emotional eating because the more shame I felt about it, the more I numbed that shame with food.

Little did I know then that this purge triggered by Charlie's disappearance after would end up being my last.

Sex Became a Way to Feel Powerful and in Control

As I briefly shared in Chapter 2, I had also smoked cigarettes since I was 16, binge drank, and partied A LOT. I took my first ecstasy pill at 19 years old and I was hooked on partying almost every weekend for years. I started going to rave parties and often took up to ten pills in a night, amongst various other concoctions of party drugs. I would sometimes blank out and not remember what I had done the previous night.

Meanwhile, I somehow managed to work in corporate jobs— as a manager or a personal assistant for law firms, accounting firms, and marketing companies.

I always had a lot of casual sex and one-night stands and had slept with most of my male friends. To me it felt like I was using these men for sex, not the other way around. This gave me a feeling of a power and control. I was the girl whose partnered-up friends were secretly worried that I would try to sleep with their partners!

That is why when I became a swinger I felt so liberated, because now my friends actually wanted me to sleep with their boyfriend!

I used Casual Dating to Avoid Being Vulnerable

Dating had also become another way to numb my pain. Although I deeply desired an emotional connection with a man, I was also deeply afraid to be hurt again. I used sex as a protection and I was casually seeing up to 10 different men at once so that I never got close to any of them.

"I'm just having fun" … I would tell myself!

But I was lying to myself. I was completely avoiding any kind of intimacy, which underneath was what I truly longed for.

This is how I had been living for 10 years ever since I left my ex-husband in New Zealand. I had been completely numbing my whole life. Except I had no idea that was what I was doing.

Every time I felt rejected or abandoned by a man I would up and leave. In truth, the person I was truly running away from was myself. The person I was abandoning was me.

I was running from the pain in my heart of not feeling lovable. Hence, why I was acting so unloving towards myself.

This treatment towards myself was reflective of my own self-hatred. The self-hatred that I was trying to purge in unhealthy ways from my emotional body.

I Was Chasing Him and Running Away From Myself

So when Charlie came into my life, he came in to show me all of this. He was showing me my self-hate. His inability to love me was reflective of the inability I was having of loving myself.

Him running away from me was simply the reflection of how I had been running away from myself. Because how could I expect him to love me and show up for me when I wasn't doing the same?

But I didn't know that then, so when he started ignoring me and becoming distant I decided that I would do my usual trick of running away and hooking up with someone else.

I was going to go to Bali and meet up with a guy I had met on an online dating site. We were going to party up the week together! I was planning to numb all my pain - yet again.

But the universe had different plans for me this time. It was finally time for me to stop running. It was time for me to face everything I had been avoiding. It was time for me to feel all the pain I had been numbing for the last ten years of my life!

You see, I felt so sure that Charlie was "the one" that when he ran away I became so confused and devastated by the whole thing that I started googling about why soulmates runaway. I was desperate to understand and know why this was happening.

How could I have this intense soul connection with him and then he ran away from me? It wasn't fair universe!

This is when I discovered … twin flames.

I Became Obsessed About this Twin Flame Idea

I had to know everything I could about this whole twin flame thing. I googled and read all the twin flame websites for hours and hours, I found facebook groups, I read forums, I watched youtube videos, I did twin flame meditations and booked in to see twin flame healers and psychics.

I became obsessed!

Everything I read was like it was written exactly about me and Charlie. One article even said "you will think that is written specifically about you and your twin flame."

If you are reading this and have had this "twin flame" experience, you will know EXACTLY the kind of obsessed feeling I am talking about and are probably nodding your head in agreement because you have done exactly the same thing.

I Thought That He Must Be My Twin Flame

The articles said that he would run away because he is so scared of the intensity of the connection, which is exactly what he said!

They said that the connection would bring up all our fears and wounds and we would have to have time apart to heal ourselves from these so we can keep coming back together.

Then every time we come back together, more wounds will come up to be healed and then we will keep doing this back and forth until we have done enough healing and will finally choose to be together.

So that is what I decided I must do then! I must heal myself and I must love myself first, so that he will then love me.

I thought that once I healed myself, then he will heal too and then he will want to be with me!

I have to look back and laugh at how funny this thought is now because the whole idea of desperately wanting someone to love me and be with me actually comes from a lack of self-love.

But I know that's what I needed to think to give me such a strong drive to heal myself.

Because it was never about him coming back to me. It was always about me coming back home to myself. This was the start of the journey to me finding my inner soulmate!

He was the catalyst of my spiritual awakening.

Letting Go of Who I Thought I Was Supposed to Be

When I couldn't actually get in contact with the other guy I was going to party up with, I started googling healing retreats in bali instead. I booked in for one in the spiritual heart of Bali— at the Yogabarn in Ubud.

From that moment my life was forever changed.

It was then that I finally saw all the ways I had been numbing my whole life and who I thought I was wasn't who I was at all!

The purging, the partying, the smoking, the drinking, the sex, the 'being busy', the overworking, the running away - it was all just me numbing myself to avoid feeling my deep emotional pain.

As Brené Brown says, I had to let go of who I thought I was supposed to be, to embrace who I am.

After two weeks of deep healing, I returned to Australia as a more awakened woman and my life would never be the same again.

I almost immediately told my mum and dad about the swinging and escorting as I had kept this part of my life a secret from them. But I was done with the hiding and having to lie about how I was making money and why I was travelling. I knew telling them the truth would set me free.

They met me with unconditional love and compassion and told me they were proud of me no matter what career I chose. My only regret was that I didn't tell them sooner, as being completely open about it only drew us closer.

In the week away I had also completely healed my eating disorder. I told my parents about that too, which liberated me from the shame I had felt and helped me to never binge or purge again.

The One Question That Changed My Life

When people ask me how I healed myself so quickly, I tell them that I just kept asking myself this ONE question - "Is this loving to myself?" when making all of my choices.

If I felt the urge to have a smoke I would ask "is this loving to myself?" and the answer was always no.

So then I would ask "Do I want this (coping mechanism) or do I want love?"

The answer was always love!

When I imagined that love I envisioned that it was Charlie's love.

I felt that I was choosing his love to come to me, but ultimately it was my own love that I was choosing.

But the want for his love was so strong that it motivated me enough to keep choosing to love and heal myself. I needed that motivation and drive back then to keep going with my conscious choices that were most loving to myself.

And eventually in time I would find that I was giving myself enough love that I didn't yearn for it to come from him anymore.

The "Twin Flame" Spiritual Awakening

Spirituality Was My New Obsession

So I had given up smoking whilst I was in Bali; I stopped taking party drugs and binge drinking. It was like I was just suddenly able to stop doing anything that was unloving to myself, even down to the food I ate. Every choice was made from asking myself "is this loving to myself?"

I was attending regular yoga and meditation classes and meditating almost every morning and night. I was obsessed with learning as much about spirituality and healing as I could. It was like a whole new world and I was going through a rebirth!

I outgrew friendships that came from being the less conscious version of me and I became close friends with healers and mentors as I became part of a big spiritual community.

I was mentored by Spiritual Navigator, Rameka Chin who helped me develop my own healing and psychic abilities. I was so surprised at how accurate my readings were and the results that people were receiving from my energy healing and reiki sessions were deeply powerful.

But I had also intuitively known that I had spiritual gifts and I always felt connected to angels. When I looked back on my life I realised that angel symbolism had been all around me; I had even named my cat Angel!

I was allowing myself to feel any emotional pain that came up and I stopped to give myself time to process my feelings. I was no longer choosing my old coping mechanisms and numbing ways, they were simply not in my reality anymore.

But I Was Still Waiting for My "Twin Flame"

Over the next 18 months Charlie would still come in and out of my life. I still felt the intense connection and desire to want to be with him each time. When he would disappear it would bring up more pain and emotions for me to feel which would send me deeper into my own healing and growth.

Even though I had thought he would start healing himself too, I started to realise that he wasn't healing at all and that he was still the same person from when we first met and that I was starting to massively outgrow him.

When we spoke I would tell him what I was learning and I often still gave my power away by going into being a rescuer. I told him how he needed to heal himself and that his wounds were just coming up for healing and that if he wanted to be with me then he would need to work on this. It was very frustrating and confusing for me when he kept running away from me instead of choosing to look at himself!

"If only he could see that if he just healed himself that we could be together in the most amazing soulmate relationship!", is what I would tell myself.

Although I was keeping busy with learning about myself, he was still in the back of my mind. I was even in a relationship with someone else at one point, I tried to settle with another man because I was so over Charlie's actions not aligning with his promises!

I was Waiting for Him to Choose Me

I would often wonder how much healing I needed to do on myself before Charlie would want to be with me! Just waiting, wishing, and hoping that one day he would turn around and choose me.

I had read on forums that some people had been waiting 20 + years for their twin flame to return; I was praying that it wouldn't happen to me!

During our times of connection he would say things like "I'm just not ready for a relationship yet, the timing with us is never quite right, when I am ready to date your door will be the first one I knock on, I need to think about my kids first" and the worst one he kept repeating was "*I don't want to hurt you.*"

To which my response was "*you already are hurting me every time you run away.*"

These words were a complete avoidance of taking ownership for what was really going on with him. He was also the reflection of the ways I was still avoiding fully feeling my abandonment and rejection wounds and not taking ownership of what had happened in my past relationships. I was also running co-dependent patterns of overgiving and rescuing with him. Even though I was doing all this spiritual self-love work I was still giving my power away to someone who wasn't available and I couldn't understand why!

#LOVEPRACTICE: IS THIS LOVING TO MYSELF?

Write up on a piece of paper the words "Is this Loving to Myself?"

Put this on your fridge, on your bathroom mirror, in your bedroom, in your car, near your computer, on the back of your phone, on your screensavers! As many places as possible!

This is to remind you to continually be asking "is this loving to myself?" It could be as simple as choosing what to eat or saying no to someone who asks you to hang out with them when you know that you need time for yourself.

It could be choosing to wake up and meditate instead of getting on your phone. It could be getting into nature first thing in the morning or getting up and exercising instead of staying in bed. It can be saying no when a part of you wants to say yes, but you know that it isn't going to serve you in the long term!

This is not based on what you think you "should" do based on what other people have said or based on a fear, such as what people might think or that you might miss out on something else if you choose the other option.

This is about tuning into your own heart and asking it what would be the most loving choice.

If you struggle to get an answer, close your eyes, put your hand on your heart, breathe in deeply and ask "what would be the most loving thing to do for myself?"

If you still don't get an answer, just choose something and trust that it will be exactly the one for you. Don't worry about getting it perfect each time, it is all part of the learning, and be self-compassionate if you think you made the wrong choice and just know that what you needed to get was the learning and growth.

I don't think there is any such thing as a wrong choice if you get the lesson from it. You will always know if you didn't honour yourself in that choice because you will feel some kind of contraction, icky feeling inside, upset, or things just won't seem to flow. Loving choices always feel expansive.

You can also ask yourself; "Does this feel expansive or contractive in my body?"

Each time you ask yourself these questions you are getting to know yourself more. You are connecting to your heart and tuning into your body and doing this will slowly change how you feel about yourself and the answers will come more easily over time.

Shifting into the Energetic Vibration of Love

All of the small self-loving choices you make each day add up and affect your vibration. The more you choose what is most self-loving the more your vibration becomes higher and then the easier it becomes to just do these things naturally. Until eventually you can't not do the self-loving choice, it's become part of who you are and you wouldn't choose it any other way.

On my birthday a few months after my spiritual awakening I tried to smoke a cigarette. I took one puff and threw it out, ran to the bathroom to scrub my mouth out from the foul taste. It was the worst thing I had ever tasted in my life. I could literally feel all the chemicals, it was gross! I knew that I would never have a smoke again, because I was no longer a vibrational match for it and my body would simply not allow it.

So the higher you vibrate the less you become an energetic match for the things that don't serve you and then the more you attract all the love and abundance that your heart desires. Every time you make a choice to love you, the more you attract love, because you attract what you are. If you want love, you be and act from a place of love and then you will have love!

#LOVEBOMBS: CREATING BOUNDARIES

The previous self-love practice is a great way to start discovering and implementing your boundaries. The more you say no to what doesn't serve you, the more you say yes to what does!

The first boundaries you set are the ones you create with yourself, so the better you get with creating and following them, the better you will be able to set them with other people. Your boundaries are ultimately what helps you live inside your integrity and values and living inside your values is actually what makes you happy—so having boundaries in place is vital to your happiness!

#LOVEGIFT: THE V.I.B.E. CIRCLE BOUNDARIES TRAINING

I can't stress the importance of boundaries enough so I really wanted to dive a bit deeper with you into knowing and discovering your boundaries.

In this training I will share with you my V.I.B.E. Circle - where Values, Integrity and Boundaries equal your Experience of life. Through this bonus training you will discover your boundaries based on your values and set your integrity to live inside that, which then sets you up to experience living life inside of your values.

You can get immediate access to this by going to www.ejlove.com/vibecircle

Chapter 8

Are You Ready for The One?

"When you call in "the one", you will be shown everything inside of you that needs to be brought into love"

One day I realised that there was a book in all the texts, notes, and letters I wrote to Charlie over that time about my healing—especially when I uncontrollably went into rescuer mode telling him how he could heal himself!

When I collated them all together I had written over 50,000 words!

Some of it I sent to him, most of it I kept for myself just to get out what was coming up for me. Looking back now even though I thought it was meant for him, it was really the message that my own soul needed to hear.

Of course back then I thought he was the "*other half of my soul*"!

So off I travelled back to Bali for two months to write this book!

I wrote about every relationship and heartbreak that I had in my childhood and then in my adult relationships, both in friendships and in my romantic relationships with men. I wrote about how they made me feel, how I reacted, and how it impacted me and my choices.

This is when I started to have huge "aha" moments and I saw some very clear patterns that I had been playing out.

But I hadn't quite discovered how to shift these yet! I will be taking you through discovering and shifting your patterns in chapters 11-19.

By the end of the two months in Bali I was so close to finish writing that book.

It was 72,338 words long and it had 20 chapters. I had just finished writing Chapter 18 which was called "Soulmates" where I explained the different types of soulmates based on my own experiences with what I thought back then were twin flames and karmic soulmates.

The one thing I hadn't written about was becoming my own soulmate though. That's because I hadn't got there myself yet! I didn't even know that was a thing; I always thought a soulmate was someone else, not me!

So it was no wonder I never got past this chapter and how that chapter, in fact, is now a whole book—the very book that you are reading.

I Finally Let Him Go

I spoke to Charlie a few times whilst I was in Bali about my initial book. He knew he was going to be in it and he said he was excited and wanted the first copy! The last time we spoke he told me he was moving back to New Zealand to be with his children. I even considered for a moment the possibility of moving back there to try and be with him, even though he clearly didn't want to be with me!

But in my heart I knew that we would never be together. It was time to let him go for good and to stop hoping he would choose to be with me.

He wasn't available and I couldn't keep doing this to myself.

When I got off that last phone call with him, I wept for three hours as I felt the grief of the rejection surface. This was really just the beginning of healing years of rejection and abandonment wounds.

The Twin Flame Journey Was Never About Him

What I eventually came to learn was that the twin flame journey was all about self!

It was never really about him, it was about letting go of the idea of him. It was letting go of the idea that I needed a man to complete me, letting go of this childhood dream I had attached myself to, letting go of the "happily ever after" fairy tales I grew up on.

The yearning I felt for him was the yearning I felt for getting love from a man, as though this was what I needed to validate my worthiness to exist. It was also linked to the times my father wasn't around and I was now trying to get his love from another man. I had actually been unconsciously doing this my whole life with men!

But the only way I was going to get this was by continuing to give this love to myself every day, to be my own parent and partner first. To have my inner masculine show up and be present for me.

Even though I was on the self-love path, what I didn't know then was that there was so much more to go … far out …yes … there is always more!!

I had been doing all this spiritual kind of self-love work, but I hadn't gone deep enough into my wounds, my shadows, my co-dependent ways of outsourcing love and safety. I didn't even know what co-dependency really was! I didn't know that I was playing out roles of rescuing, caretaking, people pleasing and martyring myself in relationships!

I hadn't actually consciously worked on healing my past relationships with men. Even though I had healed myself from most of my unhealthy numbing ways, what I now needed to look at was how I had been showing up in these relationships and given my power away trying to get love from them.

However, I thought I had that shit sorted now that I was like so "*awake.*" Oh, but how much more awakening there was going to be!

Little did I know that it was going to take another woundmate for me to awaken to all the shit I still had around men!

Another woundmate to show me that I was being co-dependent as fuck!

I Started "Calling In The One"

But instead of focusing on healing my past relationships, I decided that I would now … wait for it … start "calling in my soulmate."

With Charlie out of the picture, I decided I needed to be open for someone who was ready and available to me. I thought it was all about Charlie not being ready and that I was open to love and he wasn't … ummm …

Now we all know how that ended up, don't we?!

Even though I wasn't consciously "healing my relationship with men," when I started "calling in my soulmate" I would call in someone who would show me all the shit I need to heal around men!

Because how could I attract "the one" when I had all these unconscious blocks and bullshit stories about love and men, such as "it's not safe to be loved" and "all men are bastards and liars" …

Plus I still had a giant energetic fuck-off wall built around my heart towards men.

Are You Ready for The One?

Even though I thought I loved men, boy oh boy, was I in for a rude yet, necessary awakening!!

And once I started calling this in, the universe delivered smart quick!

Just one month later after consciously manifesting and visualising him every day, Leo came steamrolling into my life.

He was exactly as I had pictured him and he was saying all the words I had longed to hear from Charlie. He even wanted to be in a relationship with me straight away, unlike Charlie who was still "not ready" after 18 months!

I honestly thought I had now manifested something amazing … I thought *shit, I'm so freaking good at this whole manifesting thing!*

But I was manifesting from a place of scarcity, not from a place of already being the soulmate I desire. I was trying to manifest something to fill up what I felt was missing, rather than matching the abundance of love that I already feel.

So what did the universe deliver me?

Someone who would reflect back to me all the places where I didn't feel like "the one", so I could call myself back to oneness. To help me see all of those parts that I was trying to fill up, all my voids. This was so that these disowned parts of myself could be seen and brought into love, bringing me into the wholeness that I was actually calling in.

Because when I "called in the one," I was calling in myself. Because I was the one I had been waiting for, I just didn't know it yet!

Whatever I was judging, unloving, disowning, or shaming in me was going to be shown to me in another human being, in this woundmate.

> **#LOVEBOMB: CALLING IN YOUR SOULMATE**
>
> Let this be a heads up to you when you try calling in a soulmate from a place of lack and before you have healed from your past relationships: the thing that the universe will do is bring situations and people into your life to show you all the blocks and wounds that you still hold to having this soulmate relationship you are calling in.
>
> Because when you call in love, the universe will show you everything that has not been brought into love yet! So then you can bring attention to these places and find ways to love them.

You Need to Become Your Own Soulmate First

This is why when I was calling in the one, the universe delivered me an intense, toxic relationship with the man who would trigger my core wounds and show me all the shit that I still didn't love about myself and all the ways I was giving my power away trying to get love from outside of myself.

It was then up to me to decide whether to choose to heal those wounds or to avoid looking at them and stay stuck in what seemed like a never-ending, repeating cycle of emotional pain and co-dependent relationships.

Since you are reading the very words in this book you know that I chose the first option.

Making this choice is where instead of calling in your one, you become your own one first. It is then from this place that you can naturally attract soulmate energy. Because you are not searching for a soulmate, you have found your inner soulmate and now you are simply BEING your soulmate.

Then you become an energetic match for other people who are being their own soulmate too. These are the kinds of healthy relationships that will flourish and grow into something beautiful, honouring, and often long lasting.

Unfortunately, these connections don't usually seem as exciting and intense as woundmate relationships at first and you may not even recognise them!

This is because of the romantic conditioning and beliefs taught to us around what a soulmate and twin flame relationship should look like and feel like and if something isn't that intense you may even discount it!

We are going to look at how to know if someone is a soulmate, woundmate, or twin flame in chapters 9 and 10!

#LOVEGIFT: THE MAP TO "THE ONE"

I have created something super special here for you. This is a map that outlines so much of what is in this book, so if you are a more visual person you can see how everything interlinks. You can download it by going to www.ejlove.com/theonemap. It is one of my best tools that explains co-dependency and I go into it in further detail in my online program and workshops.

Chapter 9

"Twin Flames" and Narcissism

"The purpose of a "twin flame" coming into your life is to help you to heal your co-dependency so that you can see that YOU are your true twin flame."

There is just one more thing you need to know about Charlie and this is the clincher, so hold onto your seats and pants!

Unlike I did ;)

I Found Out the Truth About My "Twin Flame"

Two months into the relationship with Leo I received a message on Facebook from the woman Charlie was now in a relationship with in New Zealand. He always told me that they were just friends; I often had my suspicions, but always gave him the benefit of the doubt.

In her message she asked me if I had ever been intimate with Charlie because she had been in a long-distance relationship almost the whole time he was in Australia and she was now four months pregnant!

I hopped on a phone call with her and the first thing she said was "I've been given a list of 10 women's names to call from one of Charlie's friends, your name is at the top of that list."

After an hour of chatting we discovered that he had lied to both of us about each other and that he had used exactly the same wording, stories, and lines on both of us. I could imagine it was extremely painful for her to hear this. I assumed that he had done the same thing with every woman on that list. This was his harem of women that he kept leading on to feel good about himself.

So he was never someone who wasn't ready to be with me, he was someone who was dating lots of women at once and telling all of them the same stories and lies. He was never scared of the intensity of our connection, he was afraid he would get caught and he enjoyed the supply he got from me chasing him.

I Was Just His Narcissistic Supply

When I say narcissistic supply, what I mean by this is that this feeds the narcissist's need for attention, admiration, and approval to which keeps up their false self. Narcissists present a completely false self to the world because they are so deeply insecure and it would be like emotional death for anyone to see the real them.

Think of it like a movie where the evil genius needs to take energy from people to keep his strength up or else he dies. That's what a narcissist is like, they need this supply to survive. Most of them have no idea that they even have a false self, they think this is who they are and this is why they are so easily able to fool people, because they believe their own lies.

So I wasn't really the most amazing woman he had ever met. I was just narcissistic supply to him and he had been lovebombing me and then discarding me and I was only egging it on with the way I was obsessively behaving about being with him.

It was so hard for me to even believe that someone could be like this, but it was also a big relief to know that I had let that connection go. However, I still felt like a bit of a fool, I could not believe that I had obsessed for 18 months over this guy who was just a pathological liar and manipulator!

But back then I wasn't thinking or seeing things properly, because I always chose to see the good in people and it never crossed my mind that he would be lying to me, especially when his sob stories about his ex-partner cheating on him and how he was scared to fall in love again were so convincing.

Discovering the Exhibitionist Narcissist

Eventually I would learn that he was an exhibitionist narcissist. An exhibitionist narcissist is the type of narcissist that most people think of when they hear the word "narcissist." But narcissism is a spectrum, which includes everything from having narcissistic traits (which everyone has to some degree) to having NPD—Narcissistic Personality Disorder.

There are many types of narcissists and here I'll share about the three main types of narcissists that I have personally experienced. The exhibitionist type of narcissist is someone who wants to get attention and be adored. They have a sense of entitlement and they will brag about their achievements. Even though they appear to think they are better than other people, underneath that lies their deep insecurities that they cover with a false mask of entitlement.

Charlie would often go on about his amazing business ideas and grandiose projects and he would talk about how everyone looked up to him because he was such a leader amongst his friends. I thought he was just being proud of his success, but when I really sat with what he said it was obvious that he was putting his friends down and bragging about himself.

His words never seemed to matched up with his actions and his friends had even tried to tell me that he was a player, but I didn't listen. None of his ideas ever came to fruition and his current partner told me that she had been the one supporting him financially.

Little did I know then that whilst I was discovering all of this about Charlie and berating myself for not seeing this earlier, I was going through something very similar with Leo, except it would be much, much worse. What I would later find out was that Leo was a covert narcissist. They are even harder to pick, more manipulative, and this makes them far more dangerous.

I Was Under the Covert Narcissist's Spell

This is why when I was reading about what a narcissist was, it didn't seem like Leo. He didn't fit the criteria of a stereotypical narcissist. If anything, he appeared to be more insecure and private than full of himself. It wouldn't be until long after that relationship ended and I came out of the dusty haze that I would realise that I was under a covert narcissist's manipulative spell.

A covert narcissist wants to be special, but they are more insecure so instead of making themselves appear to be special, they choose to attach themselves to people and items that make them special by association.

This is why powerful, successful women like me are prime targets for covert narcissists. Because a covert narcissist will see that by being associated with you, they will then be seen as special. This is why initially I was pedestalled and idealised by Leo.

He saw me like this shiny object of narcissistic supply that he could be associated with. He would always talk me up to other people, go on about my achievements, and tell everyone how amazing I was. It felt like he was just being proud of me, but really he was doing this to be seen as special because he was with me.

This was until the first devaluing stage began.

A covert narcissist will also get narcissistic supply in a way that is less obvious. This includes gaslighting, where they say one thing and do another or put the blame on you and try to make you question yourself to feel like you are the crazy one. They will completely make up things you have said or twist words around to make you sound like you are the one in the wrong.

They will find out your deepest insecurities and vulnerabilities and use them to deliberately trigger you because they get a kick out of it. Your reactions will simply give them more supply and then they make out like they are the victim in all of it and you then get all the blame.

They also tend to have a split personality. This is where everyone in the outside world sees them as this kind, loving person, but behind closed doors they turn abusive and nasty. This is why it can be so hard for others to even see what is going on or to even believe that person could act that way.

Yep, covert narcs are so dangerous because they are so hard to spot.

The Pure Evil Toxic Narcissist

Then there was Anthony who I had met a few years earlier, right before I started escorting. We met on a swinger's website and he did the usual play-the-victim trick, making out that he had a crazy ex-partner who he needed to get away from. Me, being the rescuer of course, invited him to stay in my house that my boss had rented out to me and I gave him a job at the gym I was managing.

But within a few weeks he turned into a horrible, nasty monster and started behaving really oddly. Such as putting a hidden program on the computers so he could screen record everything I was doing and get all my passwords. Sending naked photos to my friends and hanging out with one friend and saying things to try and pit us against each other. Telling my swinging friends obvious lies about me, including that I used to be a man! Like, what the actual fuck?!

It was even his suggestion that led me into the sex industry. He suggested that I should become an escort and that he would be my driver and security so that he could make money off me. I never went ahead with that idea then, but it planted the seed for what would come next.

When I didn't give him the supply he wanted, he started threatening to take me down. He told me that he was going to take my job and my home away from me. I had no idea what I had done to him to deserve this, all I had tried to do was help him get back on his feet.

When I asked him what I had done to him and why he was being like this, all he kept saying was "you just think you are all that." Which made no sense to me at all. He was never willing to sit down and talk about it, it was like he hated me and was out to get me for no real reason. It was so confusing for me!

He started to schmooze up to my boss and was manipulating him too.

He then kept saying to me about my boss, "I'm going to take him for all he is worth."

He Flipped My Life Upside Down

I tried to tell my boss, but he wouldn't believe that Anthony could even be like that, because he had him wrapped around his little finger! Eventually he managed to turn my boss against me too. He believed everything Anthony had said about me, including telling him that I was now an escort and therefore "it wouldn't look good if I was managing the gym."

My living situation was now unbearable so I moved out, left the job, and even though I already had three job offers to manage other gyms, that's when I actually started working full time as a private escort.

Once I had left my home I cut all contact with him. I felt completely free in my new life and we never spoke again. He had got want he wanted - my job, my car and my home!

A month later I met another exhibitionist narcissist through escorting and got blindsighted again with my rescuing and empathetic ways.

Looking back I realised that I had actually experienced all three different types before I even met Charlie! But back then I didn't even know that narcissists existed. I didn't know that narcissism was even a thing that I needed to be wary of, I just thought all people had empathy. I gave my trust to people so quickly.

So the toxic narcissist is extremely destructive. They love chaos, they love creating drama whilst often claiming "I hate drama." They want the attention and they will try to make you feel inferior to them. They get their supply by hurting people and getting off on their fear. It's like entertainment for them to see people fall after building them up, like it's just one big, sadistic game to them. They will have no hesitation destroying your career, your home, your relationships, and your whole life, they actually gain their energy from it.

Could You Be a Narcissist?

I hope this has helped you to identify if you have experienced any of these types of narcissists. You may have even recognised some narcissistic traits in yourself and are questioning if you may be a narcissist! The main thing to know is that narcissists have not developed the part of their brain that has empathy.

If they show empathy, it is only used as manipulation. So if you feel any kind of empathy for others then you can rest assured that you are not a narcissist!

Phew!

Like me, you may now be wondering why the hell you kept attracting these damn narcissists? In chapter 13 on Narcissists, Empaths, and Co-Dependents I will give you a full understanding of this and take you through a powerful healing process so that you will be unlikely to attract one again!

I am also going to take you deeper into understanding the phases of idealisation/lovebombing, devaluing, and discarding, as well as the main red flags and signs to watch out for. I could write a whole other book on that!

Make sure you are following me on YouTube and Facebook as there are extra videos on narcissism. My social media links are in the resources section at the back of this book.

Is Your Twin Flame Really a Narcissist?

The main reason I want to mention this is to help you identify if someone you thought was a soulmate or twin flame is in fact a narcissist. I thought Charlie was my twin flame and Leo told me he was my twin soul. Both were narcissists, they were just different types.

I also wanted to call out here the obsessive "twin flame" chasing that is in fact a form of spiritual bypassing. This obsession with being with a twin flame that runs away or doesn't treat you right can be enabling narcissistic abuse. When you are giving your power away to them in this way you are avoiding facing the real emotional issues and wounds.

If your supposed "twin flame" is a narcissist they may even be deliberately treating you badly or running away because they know that it triggers you.

So many of my clients have come to me having been or are going through a "twin flame" connection and then discovering that the person they have been obsessing about being with is in fact a type of narcissist.

There are even some "*twin flame signs*" and "*narcissist red flags*" that say the same thing, such as having an intense fast moving connection. Because the narcissist will always move fast to secure you as their supply and tell you everything you want to hear to make you believe that you are their soulmate, including possibly even telling you that you are their twin flame!

"Twin Flames" that Are Unhealthy and Co-Dependent

There are so many different teachings about twin flames and what I am addressing here is just the kind of connection that is unhealthy and there is constant chasing/running, pushing/pulling. We need to stop using the term "twin flame" to describe a connection that is often toxic, co-dependent, and even abusive. This is spiritually bypassing an unhealthy relationship and this is seriously dangerous!

You may have said or heard things like:

"They are my twin flame/soulmate, even after they ignore me/abuse me, one day they will change, they have so much potential, they just need to heal themselves, this is part of the twin flame journey", etc.

But then nothing ever changes and it ends up in a constant, vicious cycle.

When one of my first spiritual mentors, Claire Kelly, said *"Twin Flame is always about Self"* it really rang true for me.

That means that if this person is not showing up for you, honouring you, respecting you, supporting you then you have to stop wasting your time longing for them and hoping one day that things will change. The real lesson to learn here is that you need to show up for yourself, honour yourself, respect yourself, and support yourself!

You are worthy of being shown up fully for, you are worthy of being wanted, being loved, adored, and honoured and that starts with you doing this for yourself first!

Real Twin Flame or False Twin Flame?

I have put the wording "twin flame" in quotation marks throughout this book because I am not suggesting the whole concept of twin flames is bullshit. I believe there are healthy, real twin flame connections out there and there are wonderful teachings out there on this. These teachings tend to focus on the relationship with yourself first.

I believe real twin flames are two souls coming together who have a healthy loving relationship with themselves first. They may come in and out of each other's lives, but they both do the work to evolve themselves and then come together to do great work in the world. They treat each other with respect and love and they do not put up with hurtful or abusive behaviour.

To help you identify the difference between what is real and false, if there is any kind of co-dependency, abuse or toxicity in the space, this person is not your real twin flame or soulmate, this person is a woundmate.

I truly believe that the purpose of a "twin flame" coming in to our lives is to heal the co-dependency that we have. This person is here to show us how we are being co-dependent. We then come to realise that we are our own twin flame first and foremost!

However, in saying that, woundmates can be evolved into soulmates when both people are prepared to do the work. But I wouldn't try doing that with a narcissist as they are very unlikely to change, it is simply too painful for them to remove their false mask because they don't know who they are without it, it would be like death for them.

I have heard that it is impossible for a narcissist to change, however, I don't have evidence for that. So the main thing to know is that you can never be the one to help them without it destroying you!

My strong recommendation is that if you are ever with a narcissist—do whatever it takes to get the fuck out of there as soon as you can!

Chapter 10

Soulmate or Woundmate?

"When you are trying to find a soul mate on the outer, what you are really needing is to become more aligned with your own soul first."

So let's dive a bit deeper now into understanding the difference between a woundmate and a soulmate!

Many people have confused woundmates for soulmates and they stay years in these relationships trying to make them work, but often end up going around in circles. They are the most difficult connections to recognise and the hardest to leave.

A woundmate will most likely shatter you to the very core of your soul and you won't even see it coming!

There are extreme highs to extreme lows, triggering, a rollercoaster of emotional turmoil, and what feels like your heart being burnt to the core and turned into particles of dust!

Woundmates may feel like a curse, but ultimately they are a gift, a blessing, a big message, they are a reflection of your wounds, and if you want to evolve the relationship or get off the emotional rollercoaster you have to do the emotional healing work on yourself.

Unfortunately most people don't want to see it when they are in it because they are usually completely besotted and lovestruck with all the amazing feelings of lust and intensity—and this is the first major sign of a woundmate!

Most often people only see it after they are left completely devastated and need help making sense of "what the hell just happened here?!"

Why Woundmates Are So Addictive

The deep intensity, the heightened feeling and excitement when you are with them—this is simply you on love drugs. You are drugged by oxytocin, serotonin, and dopamine and it is making you feel that "this connection is so intense." Every time you see them is like getting a drug hit!

When all those "oh so in love" feelings start so damn quickly, it is like you have known them your whole life. You will feel like you have never felt this before; hence why you may think "this is the one."

You start fantasising about how the relationship will be, maybe envisioning your wedding, the life you will have together, the things you will create, the name of your kids even, and you barely even know the person, right?

You have only just met them, so you wonder, how can you be thinking this way already?

Of course, you think they must be your soulmate then! You think this is a bit crazy to all be happening so fast, but it must be it, because the connection is just so intense!

When Polarity Shows Up as Chemistry

This is polarity, which is showing up as chemistry. This can be played out with narcissists and empaths, victims and rescuers, abusers and enablers, the immature masculine and the wounded feminine.

However, you can't see all of that because you are so blinded by the love drugs. You feel so alive. So energised. Life is so much sweeter with them in it. You now know why it never worked out with anyone else.

You have been waiting for this your whole life. It is like your fairy tale since childhood is finally coming true in real life!

You just can't get them out of your head. You can't stop talking about them. All you want to do is see them and be with them. You change your plans for them. You change your schedule to spend more time with them. You start pleasing them and meeting their needs and desires at the sake of your own.

Boundaries? What boundaries? You are like one soul with them and now you feel so complete. You cannot imagine ever being without them. You start doing almost everything together. You decide to move in together after just a short time. Well, it made complete sense of course since you were with each other all the time anyway!

Let's not forget the sexual chemistry you have, it's just so amazing, perhaps even the best sex you have ever had.

Of course it is, it's sexual polarity—it's addictive, isn't it?

One Day Something Changes

Then one day out of nowhere something changes, as the dream of who you thought was your soulmate starts to crumble and then begins that shattering of your heart into a million pieces!

Your woundmate pulls away and distances themselves and they stop feeding your happy chemical addiction.

Your serotonin level drops, because your woundmate, aka love drug, is ripped away from you. Your deepest wounds are now brought to the surface. You feel rejected and abandoned, you have never felt so much emotional pain before and you now wish that you had never met them!

Your heart aches and yearns for them. You long for your one and only—your love drug.

How Could They Do This to You?

How could such an amazing connection turn so heartbreaking so quickly?

Did your connection not mean anything to them?

Did they not feel it too?

You decide that you must do whatever it takes to fix this, because you can't bear this pain and you can't possibly imagine life without them. This is where you start giving your power away to save the relationship and prove yourself to them.

The rollercoaster begins—push-pull, on-off, highs-lows—from the loved-up feeling to the awful longing yearning for them feelings.

By not honouring yourself you are effectively saying that it's okay to be treated this way and then it will keep happening again and again. This is a constant re-wounding.

Hence the term—woundmate.

The Purpose of a Woundmate

So you have to ask yourself; when are you going to stop putting up with the emotional rollercoaster ride that you keep getting addicted to?

Because one day after being on the rollercoaster for far too long there comes a time that you decide enough is enough. You choose to stop giving your power away and you turn inside yourself. You choose to now heal these painful wounds that that person has been triggering in you repeatedly.

Because this is the purpose of a WOUNDMATE!

Then, and only then, will you be able to let go, complete this relationship, and find true love with your actual soulmate—the one inside of you.

Now I'm not saying all woundmate relationships happen like this; this is the extreme version of a woundmate and usually how people get fooled into thinking their woundmate is their "twin flame."

You can breathe a sigh of relief now, because here you are on the journey of healing your wounds and when you do this, you will be much less of a magnet for woundmates—yay!

You Can Evolve a Woundmate into a Healthy Relationship

You may even be in a relationship that started out this way and over time as you both have learned, grown, healed, and evolved it has become more healthy.

The only way that woundmates can work is if both people are willing to do the work on healing themselves. Both of you have to choose this as you are not there to heal or fix the other person. You cannot sit around waiting for someone to heal or to change either.

And sometimes you have to choose to honour yourself and walk away. Walking away may be the hardest decision but the most life changing thing you will ever do.

The Difference Between a Woundmate and a Soulmate

The first way you can easily tell the difference is by looking at how the connection started out.

A general rule is that:

Fast and intense = Woundmate

Slow and steady = Soulmate

Soulmates may even look like "boringmates" at the start. Maybe you will be friends first.

Maybe you won't even see them in that romantic way initially. Maybe one day they will just grow on you. Something will just shift and you will just see them in a different light.

You will feel a connection, but it won't feel like a full-on longing for them. There will be just a gentle, sweet contentment and a mutual respect that will turn into a deep love the more time that you spend with them. So it most likely didn't start out like a wild, crazy intensity, where you yearn to see them every minute of every day!

The difference is that when you take your time with a relationship and let it grow on its own naturally you are able to keep committed to the relationship with yourself and focus on your own interests, values and goals.

You won't give your power away trying to get their love or prove yourself. Instead, you are able to establish healthy boundaries and agreements and consciously communicate these (ideally using the tools in this book).

If the person pulls away or distances themselves and it this brings up feelings of rejection or abandonment this is the time to come back into yourself and use it as an opportunity to use the trigger healing practice. Then from that place you can have that conscious conversation with them to communicate your feelings and needs.

I have effectively designed this book in this way to give you the tools to be able to have a healthy soulmate relationship. The more you integrate all of these practices in the relationship with yourself first, the easier it will be to naturally show up that way when someone else is in the picture.

I Am My One and You Are Your One

There was once a time that I thought that idea of a "one and only" was everything I ever wanted, but after experiencing so many woundmates, the idea of a "one and only" lost its shine and lustre. I'm still very much open to the concept of soulmates, but this comes from a different place, it comes from a place of:

Soulmate or Woundmate?

"I am my one, you are your one, and then there is an *us* and sometimes we will be our ones together. I know that it may not last forever and today I choose to be with you."

And I'll keep choosing that person until I don't choose them. Because the person that I will always choose first is me!

You can see that there are three relationships in there—Me, You and the Relationship. This is how a healthy soulmate relationship could look.

Not just an all-in-one relationship jumbled up together! This is why having healthy boundaries is key in having conscious relationships.

Most of all though—slow the fuck down.

Why do you have to move so fast anyway? If that person is meant to be in your life, most likely you will have years to spend together.

As the song goes, "You can't hurry love, you'll just have to wait."

So be patient, trust, and have faith in the universe—she's got your back.

#LOVEPRACTICE: IDENTIFYING YOUR WOUNDMATES

Can you now recognise the people in your life who are or have been woundmates? *Write their names here.*

_____
_____
_____
_____

What wounds can you see that they triggered in you?

_____
_____
_____
_____

Can you see the teaching and gift of the connection and how you can now be grateful for what they brought into your life?

_____
_____
_____

Are there healthy boundaries you now need to put in place between you and your woundmate/s that will help move it into more of a healthy way of relating (*if they are still in your life*)?

_____
_____
_____
_____
_____
_____
_____
_____
_____
_____
_____
_____
_____
_____
_____
_____
_____
_____
_____
_____
_____
_____
_____

Chapter 11

The Re-Wounding

"You have to go back to the source wound and heal it at that place so that you stop being re-wounded."

Would you love to know how to not be magnetically attracted to another woundmate ever again?

Or perhaps how to evolve your current relationship to a more healthy one, with much less triggering?

It's now time to get you out of that victimised perspective and move you into that open-hearted empowerment!

This is a place that requires you to take real ownership of your past behaviour and the willingness to look at the things you may have been avoiding!

We often replay our old victimised story in love over and over in our minds; we tell this to our friends and we make it even more real and true.

As you wrote out in chapter 4 we usually make it about what the other person did to us or what they did wrong by us.

We say things like "I got dumped, she cheated on me, he left me for another woman, they didn't love me, he was an asshole, she was a psycho" or we make it about how we aren't good enough. "Nothing I did was never enough for her, I wasn't good enough for him."

Although those people may have acted in these ways, constantly using this kind of language is disempowering.

You may even have noticed how my language in the last few chapters has been from a victimised perspective as I have shared my story with you. Well, that's all about to change!

If you are wondering why I got you to write it out that way, this is because we are going to take what you wrote back then and completely flip it on its head. But I needed you to get it all out first and feel all the emotions that were sitting underneath that old story.

Changing the Perception of Your Past

Although we cannot change what happened, we can change the perspective we have on it. When you discover what part you played in the relationship, you will find that the story changes and you create a brand-new possibility for that relationship or the next relationship.

If you do not take responsibility for your part in it, you will most likely attract it all over again and keep replaying that story … eeeeek!

Or put up walls to try and avoid it!

When I wrote my story about my relationship with Leo from the victimised perspective I started to get curious about how I had managed to attract this into my life and I asked myself "where have I felt this before? Have I experienced something similar?" and then it hit me like a ton of bricks!

This story was almost identical to the relationship I had with my first partner.

The lying, the cheating, the betrayal, the other women, the abuse. Except it was ten times worse than what I had experienced the first time. Then there was the relationship after my husband too which was a similar experience, similar feelings, and similar stories. Although the men were all quite different personalities, the story always ended up with me

The Re-Wounding

feeling betrayed, rejected, abandoned, and unwanted. This then kept showing up over and over again in my life in all different ways.

I realised that Leo was a re-wounding from never healing myself from my first heartbreak and from childhood wounds. I now had the opportunity to go back to the source wound and heal it at that place so that I would stop being re-wounded. I had to allow myself to feel the pain that was still held within my cellular memory and the trauma that had been stored in my body for all those years.

Associating Love and Abuse as the Same Thing

As I started to dig deeper into the feelings of rejection, betrayal, and abandonment and where this stemmed from I saw so many memories as a child where I also felt this way.

It is often assumed that if someone experiences abuse in adult life that they must have been abused as child.

Although this is often the case, I never considered myself to be abused as a child as I had what I felt was a very loving childhood and was well cared for by my parents. The closest physical abuse was getting smacks on the bum from my dad as a punishment for doing something naughty. Back then this was very accepted as a way to discipline children; however, times have changed since then. But something like that could have affected how my brain associated love and it may have associated love with being smacked. It may have associated love with being physically hurt.

I remember the feeling I got when I knew my dad was angry and coming to smack me. I would try running away to hide in my room, but he would come after me and I would be saying "I'm sorry" over and over whilst he was smacking me. It never lasted long, it was a few smacks, and they weren't hard enough to do any lasting physical damage.

But I will never forget the fear I felt in my body just before he was about to smack me; I would get this anxious feeling and freeze up. This was when I started saying "I'm sorry," hoping that it would be enough to make him not want to smack me. I thought that if I apologised he would know I didn't mean to do what I did.

I can't remember what happened afterwards, but my dad was an affectionate man and it is likely that I received a hug from him at some stage to make it all better, which would have made me then feel loved.

What I perceived this to mean was that if I do something wrong, I will get punished with physical pain. That even if I say I'm sorry it won't be enough to stop it happening and there is nothing I can do about it. Then after that hurt I will get to receive love through physical touch.

So there is then an association with physical pain and love, that somehow pain leads to or precedes love or even that love is pain, or through pain is how to get more love.

I don't blame my dad, because this is cultural conditioning and he was just doing what was seen as the normal thing to do to discipline children back then.

Recognising the Pay Off

I would often hear people say that when a woman stays in an abusive relationship it is because there is some kind of pay off for her.

As I reflected on what happened with Leo. I could see the similarities around how the pain and love association played out. He would accuse me of doing something wrong. I would go into defending myself which would lead into a fight. I would feel exactly the same kind of fear in my body and go into feeling like that scared little girl again.

He would start abusing me verbally and physically. I would be apologising to try and stop him from hurting me, even if I hadn't done the thing he accused me of. Eventually once he got tired or I stopped reacting then we would come back together and have a cuddle and a kiss and I would receive what felt like love.

So there was a pay-off here for me. The pay-off for staying in the relationship and going back to him is that I would get that love after experiencing the abuse. My happy chemicals would be at a high when I was getting the cuddles from him and physical touch was also how I was shown love as a child. I unknowingly had become addicted to the love I received after the abuse.

My Brain Was Choosing What Was Familiar

My brain was choosing what had become familiar to me from what I had experienced in my childhood and in my past relationships. Even though logically I knew what was happening wasn't safe or healthy, I couldn't explain why I kept going back. The survival part of my brain was just choosing from what it thought was safe and I was chemically bonded and addicted to this cycle.

Even though the safest thing was to actually leave, the part of my brain that is built for survival doesn't think this way. Because I was living in so much fear most of the time, I was not in the part of my brain that thinks logically. I just kept going back and punishing myself and somewhere in there I was also subconsciously telling myself that I deserved it. That it was my fault that he was being this way and that I needed to be the one who changed my behaviour so he didn't hurt me anymore.

But that's actually not what was true. What was true is that I was with an unhealthy man who I had attracted based on my wounds and I was being re-wounded and that the only way to stop this was to value and honour myself by leaving and then healing myself from the wounds he was triggering.

For people who have experienced abuse as a child what often happens is that they associate love with abuse and often unconsciously associate them as being the same thing; hence why when they are calling in and manifesting love, abuse then keeps showing up over and over for them.

Can you see what you have been choosing as familiar?
_____
_____
_____
_____
_____

What has been the pay off for you?
_____
_____
_____
_____
_____

What has this been costing you?
_____
_____
_____
_____
_____

What can you see that you could have associated love with from your childhood experiences?
_____
_____
_____
_____
_____

The Re-Wounding

> **#LOVEBOMB: WHAT LOVE REALLY IS**
>
> If you are calling in a true love relationship, but have a subconscious imprint that love and abuse are the same thing, then abuse will keep showing up.
>
> This goes for anywhere that you have associated love as looking and feeling a certain way.
>
> What's love really then?
>
> You.
>
> You are love.
>
> You don't need to get love.
>
> Because it's already here.

Why Don't You Just Leave Then?

When you say to someone who is in an abusive relationship "why don't you just leave?" it is not as easy as that. I really wish it was, but it's not. The best thing you can do for someone in an abusive relationship is to try to understand their reality, be compassionate and empathetic for where they are at and how hard it must be for them to leave. Check in with them and simply ask if they need any support and let them know you are there for them without judgement of their choices.

Then be there for them when they eventually do decide to leave. This is when they will really need you to support them. If someone doesn't have that support then they are far more likely to stay in the abusive relationship.

#LOVEPRACTICE: RECOGNISING YOUR RE-WOUNDINGS

Reflect on what you wrote in your victimised perspective in chapter 3. Start to see if you can notice similarities between them and other people and relationships from your past. Particularly looking at childhood experiences and relationships, relationships with parents, friendships, and romantic relationships.

Does this person remind you of any relationships, feelings, and experiences you have had in the past? *List them here.*

_____

_____

_____

_____

_____

_____

_____

_____

How can you see that these have impacted and shaped you and your life?

_____

_____

_____

_____

_____

_____

Chapter 12

The Rescuer and the Victim

"The medicine for the one who plays the rescuer is to fully own and love their inner victim"

Exploring relationship patterns is one of my favourite things to take my clients through. When I go through these different patterns at my workshops and in 1:1 sessions there are always massive "ahas" and breakthroughs, so it makes me super excited to be able to share this with you. I hope you get few lightbulb and *facepalm* moments here too!

So in the next few chapters I am going to take you through the most common relationship patterns that I have identified with all of my clients; I know there are more though!

As you read through each one, you may notice you have played out all of them at some time or another and been on both sides of the patterns.

When you identify your patterns you will really start to see how you have been the source of your experiences. Oh yes, it can often be icky to look at the part we played in creating our own pain and suffering!

I'll tell you a "not so secret" secret—I have experienced all of these patterns too! So please be gentle on yourself, you are only human after all.

Come Here and Let Me Fix You

Playing the rescuer ... the story of my life!

Let me rephrase that: "This WAS the story of my life."

It seemed that I was a magnet for people who had so many issues going on in their lives. It was like there was some kind of big neon sign on my forehead that said "*come here and let me fix you!*"

I would find myself taking on the mother role in most of my relationships where I was the one who provided financially. It was as though I was looking after my very own child. It seemed that I always had to be the responsible one, having to look after the one who I felt needed fixing—the one who consistently played the victim. The broken one.

But the truth was that I thrived on playing the rescuer and the other person loved being a victim and so when we came together it was a full-on magnetic attraction and there was just "oh so much chemistry"—yep woundmate!

We were polarising each other as we both played out these opposite roles and fed on the highs!

I Was Enabling Victim Behaviour

One of my biggest complaints about Leo was that he never took responsibility for anything and always blamed me and everyone else for his problems. However, I was being overly responsible from the start of our relationship and I was constantly enabling his victim behaviour. I had never created space for him to step up and take responsibility, because I was always taking care of everything for him. For me, this is what felt safe. It's what I had seen my mum do for everyone as she was always taking charge and looking after everything and being the responsible one.

I thought that if I didn't organise and do things then no one else would and I didn't trust men to make big decisions or get things right or do things the way I liked them!

The Strong Independent Woman Who Doesn't Need a Man

As a "strong independent woman" I was used to doing everything myself. I was used to being in control because it made me feel safe and powerful. I was using this as a way to protect myself from being hurt by men and avoiding the feeling of deep unworthiness that I felt inside of me. By constantly doing, helping, and giving, I felt valuable.

So I didn't even give men a chance to lead, take responsibility, or make decisions. When men did help me or try to give to me I struggled to receive it or I pointed out what was wrong instead of appreciating their effort.

Or I felt like I would owe them something and, that I would have to give something back to make it even.

I didn't want that expectation on me.

I also made it mean that men thought I couldn't do things myself and I wanted to show them that I didn't really need them because I didn't want to appear needy.

The disempowering thought pattern also here was "I can't receive help because that creates dependence and it's not safe for me to rely on anyone but myself."

On top of all this is that being independent appears to be far more valued in society than having to rely on anyone. Women instinctually adapt themselves to what appears to be more valuable, so this is another reason why someone who is trying to appear independent will find it difficult to receive help.

It takes a real willingness to be vulnerable, to let your "Mr/Ms Independent" mask drop and be seen in that.

There can be a lot of vulnerability around receiving and this is common for people who have been abused as children. Often they have associated receiving with something unwanted and hurtful, therefore they do not often feel safe to receive.

> **#LOVEPRACTICE: THE VULNERABILITY OF RECEIVING**
>
> *Some questions to ponder and journal on…*
>
> Who are you if you take the "strong, independent woman" mask off?
>
> What is possible when you stop doing, giving, helping, pleasing, and proving yourself to be of worth?
>
> What if the greatest gift you could give someone was the joy you express that comes when you receive from them?
>
> What if you allowed yourself to receive love without feeling the need to do or give something to get it?

Allowing a Man to Help

I have since discovered how much healthy men really love helping and giving to a woman for no reason other than to make her happy!

I could almost not quite believe how much men loved this and how the more a woman received his help, the more it made him feel like a man and the more he felt attracted to her.

I realised that it wasn't about me not being able to do things for myself or appearing "needy," it's that I could do it all myself and a man knew that, but when he did things for me that he wanted to do it allowed me to relax and be more feminine, which made him feel more masculine.

This was like some big secret that I wish I had known my whole life! I had spent so much time and energy on trying to prove how valuable I could be to a man by all the ways I was helping him and giving to him, yet, the men who were healthy wanted to give to me and help me and then apparently they would like me more—huh?!

This was so confusing for the immature masculine part of myself that was driven to prove myself by constantly doing and providing.

I felt like I had got it completely around the wrong way and here I was trying to be the man all the time! Then I would get resentful about doing everything myself, I wanted a man to "step up." I often blasted them for not doing enough, but I was the one who never let them help and hardly ever appreciated them when they were trying to help me. This would often end up with a man becoming resistant and resentful towards me and I would end up pushing them away. This is how I ended up with men who were more in their wounded feminine energy, because I was more in the immature masculine energy. My energy wasn't even allowing in healthy integrated men.

Can you see how you may have been not allowing a man to help you?

Devaluing Myself By Overproviding and Overgiving

The main conflict I saw my parents having was about money and I unconsciously decided that I needed to make sure that I had money and looked after the finances so that a man wouldn't have anything to fight with me about!

But of course it didn't work like that and we always ended up fighting about money – it was what was familiar for my brain! I became sick of being the one who was supporting them, even though I had said to them "don't worry, I'll support you" when they left their jobs.

I would suppress the resentment and it would come out when we fought and then I would go back to paying for everything when we were on good terms. So I kept enabling this by continuing to provide and support them and not setting any boundaries around money.

I could also see it was a way to feel like I had some kind of worth and control because I didn't feel worthy unless I was giving something, which is why I had been such an overgiver my whole life. I wanted desperately for these men to love and want me and I thought that if I gave them something that I would be of value to them. I was also unconsciously creating dependency on me, so that they would be less likely to leave me…and therefore I would be safe.

In an ironic twist though, people don't actually value something unless they have earned it, especially men, and they love a challenge. Ultimately they value the most what they have to work the hardest for! So my overgiving tendencies often completely backfired on me because the more I overgave, the less they valued it and me!

Can you see how you may have been overgiving and overproviding to feel valuable?

The Medicine for Emasculation

In The Queen's Code by Alison Armstrong she speaks to how women unconsciously emasculate men. However, I believe that we are all emasculating each other and ourselves and this gets reflected back to us in our relationships.

The medicine for this is—receptivity and appreciation, initially by learning to give to and appreciate ourselves first.

Having the willingness to receive from a man, especially when it feels edgy and vulnerable.

So please, please, please let a man help you and when he does, appreciate the hell out of him for it!

A man won't want to continue to give to you and help you if he's not appreciated, especially if it then becomes an expectation instead of a gift for you. Let him know that his effort is noticed and tell him how it makes you feel, especially when it makes you happy!

Always let a man know how he makes you happy.

And if he doesn't make you happy or is not putting in any effort at all then that is a sign to leave or to both work on the relationship.

But if he is a healthy man try some appreciation first and see what happens; you might be sweetly surprised at how suddenly starts putting in more effort!

"No Matter What I Do It's Never Enough for Her"

One of the biggest complaints I hear from my male clients is "no matter what I do it never seems to be enough make her happy."

What they are really saying is that they aren't feeling appreciated for what they are already doing or that their help isn't being seen or received.

The reason why women don't often see or appreciate men is because they often assume a man is misbehaving. They assume that he should be doing things how she would do it and if he doesn't then he is doing it wrong. They focus on what he's doing wrong instead of what he's doing right.

What's underneath that is that a woman is constantly looking to find proof that a man really loves her. Instinctually she is constantly testing him to make sure that he won't leave her and that he will stay to protect her, especially when she doesn't feel safe.

Ironically the very reason most men leave a woman is because she is unconsciously testing him in this way!

So the more you give yourself your own love and make yourself feel safe first, the less you will put expectations on a man to show up in a certain way to prove his love to you. From this place he will show his love authentically, not from a place of feeling like he has to prove himself.

This is why appreciation is SO important. I can't stress this enough!

Alison Armstrong says that appreciation gives men more energy, it fuels them to give even more.

Appreciate. Appreciate. Appreciate.

And remember appreciate yourself while you are at it!

> **#LOVETIP: UNDERSTANDING MEN**
>
> Read the book *The Queen's Code* by Alison Armstrong—this was an absolute gamechanger in understanding men and the way I had unconsciously emasculated them and myself. I recommend that everyone read this book!

The Drive to Prove Your Worth

Often when I advise someone to ask for what they need, they ask "but then doesn't that make me look needy?"

This connects in with the appeared value of independence and needing to prove that you don't need anything from anyone and can make it on your own. Which again all comes from safety and trying to prove your worth.

Actually it sounds a bit silly, the whole "proving your worth" thing, because in actual fact if you felt worthy then you would never feel the need to prove anything to anyone. The very action of needing to prove yourself comes from a feeling of worthlessness.

I wonder what would happen if you just stopped trying to prove anything at all?

And just showed up completely as you are.

Wouldn't it be a fun experiment to sit back and notice all the things you do to try and prove your worth and not do them!

Why not try it for a week and see what happens?

The Rescuer and the Victim

Appearing "Needy" and Asking for What You Need

We are conditioned that it is a bad thing if we need anything from anyone; it's as though it makes you less of a person to ask for help.

There is a form of unhealthy "neediness" that the victim role takes on, where the person relies on another person to meet their needs, rather than learning how to self-source their needs and give themselves their own love first.

Neediness also appears when someone manipulates someone to get their needs met or they need someone to save them from having to deal with things themselves and they take advantage of someone's rescuer role!

Sometimes rescuers think they are doing a good thing by helping people, but in fact they are most often hindering that person's growth and stopping them from learning how to do these things for themselves and playing into the rescuer/victim dynamic.

A person in neediness comes from a place of "I need you to love me because I don't love myself, I need you to give me validation because I am not giving that to myself, I'm going outside of myself to get from you, instead of trying to self-source first; if you don't help me then I will be angry/upset/sad."

The need tends to come from a place of reliance, expectation, and demand.

A healthy place of asking for what you need comes from a place of "I am giving myself my own love first and I am doing the best I can to meet my needs. However I need extra support with this; are you able to help me meet my needs?"

This way you are connected to yourself first and you are asking that person if they are actually available to help you meet your needs, not asking them to do it all for you. The other person is then giving and helping authentically, not from a place of "I have to" or just doing it to keep you happy; this will just breed resentment.

This also gives the opportunity for that person, instead of rescuing or saving, to come in more as a supporter or provider because they are willing to help rather than it being an expectation or demand.

Being Needed as a Form of Power

When I was a former rescuer, I liked being needed and I was unconsciously creating the other person having some kind of dependence on my help so that they would be less likely to leave me, which included providing financially. Because if they needed me more than I needed them then that was emotionally safer for me.

Like when I asked Leo to leave, but he didn't have a job or money. I had felt responsible to have to meet his needs and support him, but then it felt like I was trapped and that I had lost my freedom; hence the resentment I had towards him.

The over-responsibility I took on was in fact an avoidance of appearing needy or like a victim. The more I avoided and judged these energies, the more they kept showing up in my relationships. Eventually the tables turned and I became the victim of the abuse and I had to be willing to appear needy and ask for help so that I could leave safely.

When I stopped judging the victim energy and neediness, it stopped showing up in my relationships. This meant I had to own it in myself!

I am going to take you into ownership in chapter 18 where we really explore owning all the energies that you avoid, judge, and resist in others. These are the very energies that you are shaming and suppressing in you. Until you own them and love them in yourself, they will keep showing up in your life through others!

Being the Rescuer to Avoid Appearing as the Victim

Part of playing the rescuer was to avoid looking at my own shit! I was avoiding people seeing any of my perceived flaws, insecurities, problems, or things I felt needed fixing in me. It's always so much easier to point out what others need to fix rather than looking inside ourselves.

Spending so much time helping others didn't leave much time to reflect on perhaps the ways I had felt like a victim too and how I had suppressed anger for many years of when I had been the victim of abuse that was still behind held inside my body screaming to be let out!

One of the reasons I kept ending up as a victim of abuse is because I needed to own the victimhood instead of rescuing everyone else. I had to own that I had been a victim and to feel the anger that I felt about that and to know that it's okay to feel that way.

That didn't mean staying as the victim, it meant expressing the raw emotions from that place as you did in chapter 5 and then owning my part in that experience as I am taking you through now. I own that I have been a victim in the past and now I thrive from empowering myself from it.

> ## #LOVEBOMB: THE MEDICINE FOR THE RESCUER
>
> The medicine to stop playing the rescuer and stop attracting people who play the victim is to own, love and stop suppressing and shaming your inner victim

Shadow Behaviours of the Rescuer:

Below are a lists of the Shadow Behaviours of both the rescuer and the victim. A shadow is generally an unconscious part of someone that has been suppressed and made wrong in childhood and the in adulthood it shows up in unhealthy ways trying to get needs met to feed it. The first step to ownership is having awareness of it. Over the next few chapters you will begin to recognise many of your shadow behaviours and how they have played out in your relationships.

- Overgiving with your time, energy, and resources
- Mothering and overproviding
- Being overly responsible
- Trying to have the power and control because you don't feel safe without it
- Focusing a lot of your time on working on the relationship and helping the other person instead of on yourself
- Creating some kind of dependency on you so they are less likely to leave you
- Abandoning your own wants and needs
- Trying to hide and avoid your own insecurities and perceived flaws and imperfections
- Avoiding looking at your own problems by focusing on theirs instead
- Avoiding appearing needy or like a victim
- Choosing someone who needs help because it makes you feel valuable and worthy
- Feeling vulnerable to receive and struggling to receive help
- Enabling the other person's victim and/or abusive behaviour

Shadow Behaviours of the Victim:

- Blaming other people—everything is always other people's fault
- Not willing to look at your part or take ownership and responsibility in a conflict or situation
- Blaming society and the world for what's wrong with it
- Complaining about how hard done by you are and everyone/the world is out to get you

The Rescuer and the Victim

- Constantly relying on other people to meet your needs
- Playing a victim of a situation to get love, care, validation, and to feel safe
- Manipulating someone to get your needs met
- Using your emotions to manipulate someone
- Deliberately trying to get attention, empathy and validation by telling your "poor me" / sob story
- Getting to play out your story of how people take advantage of you, use you, take from you, milk you for all you worth (and any other sob stories you would like to add here)
- Taking advantage of someone's kindness, rescuing, and helpful nature
- Acting like the child in polarity to the rescuer who is playing the mother role. You are trying to get looked after by the other person because you didn't get this from a parent when you were a child. Or you had an attachment to a parent and are playing it out because it is what is safe and familiar

#LOVEPRACTICE: OWN YOUR RESCUER AND VICTIM

Write out how and where you have played either the rescuer or victim role or both.

_____
_____
_____
_____
_____
_____
_____

Chapter 13

Narcissists, Empaths and Co-Dependents

"Narcissists rely on your need to be externally validated to first suck you in and then trigger your wounds to keep you there."

When I finally figured out I had been fooled by a narcissist, I felt a lot of shame… I thought that I should have known better! I questioned "how did a smart, self-aware woman like me end up in an abusive relationship?". The truth was that because I was a co-dependent and an empath, I was actually a prime target for a narcissist.

If you are any of these—successful, appear to have some kind of 'status', an empath, spiritual, attractive, intelligent, have positive energy, appear to be wealthy, run the co-dependent rescuer role—then you are a prime target for a narcissist!

This is similar to the rescuer/victim polarity because empaths tend to play the rescuer role in their relationships. They feel great empathy for another person and like to do whatever they can to help them. Not only are they polar opposites with a narcissist, which creates red-hot chemistry, but empaths find it really hard to comprehend that someone could not feel empathy; hence why the narcissist's sob story is so believable.

Narcissists to some degree know this and this makes empaths their prime targets as the empaths get hooked in by the victim role the narcissist plays.

What Are Empaths and Co-Dependents?

An empath is someone who tends to be very intuitive and will often feel the emotions and energy of others and even take on others' emotions as their own feelings. It can feel like an emotional rollercoaster at times and you can also take on unnecessary stress and physical pain that isn't yours.

Everyone to some degree is empathic, however in high spectrum narcissists that part of their brain isn't as developed.

I recommend doing a google search on empaths as there are lots of articles on the internet that will tell you the traits of an empath. Empaths are often co-dependent in relationships, but they are not the same thing.

A co-dependent, or what is now termed as someone who has self-love deficit disorder, is someone who looks outside of themselves for love and approval, because they are not giving this to themselves. Like empaths, their focus is more on outside of themselves and this is when they go into caretaking and pleasing others, rather than looking after themselves first. They will martyr themselves and put up with and enable unhealthy, toxic behaviours. This is to keep the peace and to keep receiving love and approval from the other person.

> ### #LOVETIP: CO-DEPENDENT ROLES
>
> In Sharon Pearson's book *Ultimate You* she explains in depth how we each take on different roles as children to make sure the 'magical big people' aka adults look after us. These roles lead us to either underfunction or overfunction and then we play these roles out in our relationships to keep getting love and approval. For example the rescuer, people pleaser, caretaker and martyr would be the overfunctioning roles and the victim, drama queen and robot would be underfunctioning roles. We will tend to attract someone who runs the polar opposite roles and the roles we played with our

> parents, because, again, this is what is familiar and safe for us, yet it is not who we truly are!
>
> I also created a powerful process where I help people to 'Release their Roles' so they can come back into alignment with their soul - who they truly are. Or as Sharon would say - their 'I-AMness'.

Why Lovebombing Works So Well

This is why the lovebombing phase of the narcissist (where they shower their victim with adoration) works so well, because the co-dependent is having their needs met for love and approval. This makes them feel like the narcissist loves them so much that they won't ever reject or abandon them, which are the deepest fears of the co-dependent.

But the lovebombing actually is leading them into a false sense of security, because those exact fears and wounds are triggered when the narcissist goes into the devaluing phase and the co-dependent then gives their power away trying to get back the narcissist's love and approval. This is where they start enabling the unhealthy and abusive behaviour.

What Does Enabling Abusive Behaviour Mean?

I want to be clear here with what I mean by "enabling," because this is not victim blaming. If someone has been abused, it is not the fault of the person that they have been abused. But by recognising the ways that we enable someone's behaviour it helps us to step back into our power.

What tends to happen, particularly in narcissistic abusive relationships, is that the person who initially came in as the rescuer is soon made out to be the perpetrator in the abuser's eyes. The abuser then plays out being the victim, but actually it is the rescuer that is the real victim of the abuse. The way that the victim of the abuse enables the abusive behaviour is by being the abuser's rescuer. This dynamic is called the drama triangle. You can get a copy of this diagram at www.ejlove.com/dramatriangle.

Here are the eight main ways that abusive behaviour is enabled by the co-dependent:

1. They try to "keep the peace" by going along with whatever the abuser wants and avoiding any kind of conflict that may trigger further abuse.
2. They tolerate far less than they deserve and keep going back again and again after leaving.
3. They may deny that the person is abusive and/or make excuses for the behaviour such as "they are just upset, they didn't mean it, it will be different now, they are not really like that, but it's not all the time, they will change."
4. They clean up the abuser's mess and take on the consequences of it on themselves. This includes things like paying to get items fixed that the abuser has broken.
5. Taking on financial responsibility of the abuser and paying their debts for them.
6. Not setting any boundaries and/or allowing their boundaries to be consistently crossed without any consequences.
7. Hiding themselves from public view/staying silent/isolating themselves so people don't suspect what is going on.
8. Thinking that they need to stay in the relationship so they can save the abuser and change their abusive ways or staying to prevent the abuser from hurting themselves or other people.

Signs of Co-dependency:

- All the behaviours from the rescuer pattern (see previous chapter)
- The enabling abusive behaviours above
- Often feel responsible for other people's choices and feelings and people please and overgive
- Go outside of yourself and your boundaries to be liked and wanted and to avoid conflict

- May not even know what your boundaries are or that you need to have boundaries
- Have difficulty saying "no" to people and often feel guilty if you do
- Allow yourself to be manipulated and controlled
- Lie to cover up the mistakes of others
- Have a fear of rejection and abandonment and need others' approval
- Struggle to make and trust your own decisions, often second guess yourself and question your own feelings
- Find it hard to identify and ask for what you need

#LOVEPRACTICE: OWN YOUR CO-DEPENDENCY

Write out or identify the ways that you have showed up in co-dependency:

_____
_____
_____
_____
_____
_____
_____
_____
_____
_____
_____

> **#LOVEBOMB: THE PURPOSE OF NARCISSISTS?**
>
> Someone once asked me 'what is the purpose of narcissists? Why do they even exist?'
>
> My answer to this is that the purpose of a narcissist coming into your life is to show you where you are still being co-dependent. This is so that you can wake the hell up to the ways you externally seek validation and move into becoming internally validated, where you give yourself that love and approval instead.
>
> Essentially if you aren't acting in co-dependent ways then the narcissist's tactics won't actually work because they rely on their validating you to initially suck you in and then trigger your wounds to keep you there.

How to Spot a Narcissist and Kill the Attraction

The easiest way to first spot a narcissist is if they are lovebombing and pedestalling you and trying to move things very quickly. A narcissist needs to know they can hook narcissistic supply from you fast; if not, they won't continue to waste their time and they will move on to someone else.

The second way is to trust your intuition when you feel something is off or it seems too good to be true. If alarm bells are ringing or you are questioning things then please listen up and back the fuck away; your intuition is there for a reason!

The first way to kill a narcissist's attraction to you is simply by taking things slowly. This is how most healthy relationships should start out anyway. The second way is to communicate your boundaries and stick to them. You will then see in their behaviour if they are willing to go slow and respect your boundaries.

A narcissist is highly unlikely to do this; they may say that they will but their actions will say otherwise or they may even ignore you to try and get a rise out of you to give them attention and get their narcissistic supply that way.

Tricky little fuckers, aren't they?!

If the person does respect your boundaries and is willing to take things slowly, then it's unlikely they are a narcissist or unhealthy. Below is a list of the main red flags to watch out for in the idealisation phase.

Narcissist Signs—The Idealisation Phase

1. They are very flirty, charismatic, charming, funny, the life of the party and so likeable
2. Lovebomb and pedestal you by giving you lots of attention, constant words of praise and adoration, it's as though you are the most amazing person they have ever met and they often think you are their soulmate straight away
3. Start calling you by a pet name very early on in the relationship
4. Rush into the connection and wanting to see you all the time and constant and unnecessary texting and calling
5. Mirror you through appearing to love everything that you love as they are trying to build connection and resonance. They listen to your unmet needs and they meet them to give you a false sense of security.
6. Talk badly about their ex-partner, saying things such as they are a psycho, crazy, or a liar
7. Want to know everything about you and your past which is to get vulnerable information off you to use later against you
8. Shares their own vulnerable stories with you to try and build trust so they can more easily deceive you later
9. Talk about kind things they have done for others, such as volunteering, which is to make them out to be a good, trustworthy person

10. They help you and offer to do things that a long term partner usually would so that it creates dependency and a bond with them
11. Lying and exaggerating to other people in front of you
12. Their words do not align with their actions
13. Do not respect your boundaries

After the idealisation phase is the devaluation phase before going into the discard phase. I have listed the main behaviours of these phases below.

Narcissistic Behaviours— The Devaluation Phase

1. They will have a big random outburst over a small issue, making a big deal out of what seems minor
2. Constantly criticising everything you do and insulting you. It is like nothing you do is ever going to be good enough or that you cannot do the right thing
3. Your beliefs and feelings are made out to be wrong or crazy and theirs are right and justified
4. They accuse you of lying and/or cheating with no real evidence. This is so that you are always defending yourself rather than looking at them. Usually they are doing the very thing that they are accusing you of doing
5. Often get jealous, possessive and controlling
6. Only their needs seem to matter—the world seems to revolve around them and you have to give up your needs to meet their needs
7. They may accuse you of having to do what you want or not giving them enough attention or tell you that your focus is too much on your work or other people and not enough on meeting their needs
8. Gaslighting—such as misinterpreting something you said or did or completely making up something up or twisting it

around so that it looks like you are the one in the wrong. This is so that they can be the victim and punish and control you. It is also to confuse you and make you start questioning your own sanity, thoughts, and feelings

9. Deliberately embarrassing you and shaming you in front of others
10. You are always the one at fault in their eyes, unless you try to leave them, then they will apologise and make false promises to change, which never happen long term
11. Threaten you, especially if you try to break up with them. They beg you not to leave them or play the pity card to play on your empathetic nature
12. Threatening to leave you to trigger your abandonment and rejection wounds
13. Triangulation—they compare you to someone else, perhaps another romantic interest. They deliberately try to make you jealous and make the other person out to be much better than you could ever be
14. Project their own feelings and fears about themselves onto you. Calling you selfish, fake, a fraud, a liar, a manipulator, and even calling you the narcissist. Projecting anything onto you that they are not willing to own in themselves
15. Smear campaigning—making you out to be the crazy one and making themselves out to be the victim of your abuse, particularly to the next love interest, aka their new narcissistic supply
16. Withdrawing their energy and withholding sex, intimacy, and emotional support
17. Giving you the silent treatment
18. Invading your privacy—feeling entitled to information such as going through your phone and computer
19. Entitlement—things are on their terms and at their convenience. They may also feel that they are entitled to have sex with you

20. Triggering—deliberately doing things they know will trigger you as a way to get narcissistic supply
21. They manipulate and lie to other people to pit them against you

Narcissitic Behaviours—The Discard Phase

The third and final phase is when the narcissist discards you. It may take years of idealisation and devaluing before this happens. It is usually because you are not giving them enough supply and they have lost interest. They will then either block, ghost, ignore, go to another form of supply, or withdraw from you. This is also a way to get their supply from you because they know it upsets you.

After the discard phase the lovebombing phase usually begins again before going into devaluation and eventually another discard and then this cycle happens over and over. People are often stuck in this continuous cycle for years because a trauma bond is formed and this is what makes it so hard for them to leave. This is why knowing the red flags of narcissists is so important. Healing your self-love deficit is paramount to prevent getting into this kind of relationship, and leaving one.

When I was going through the discard phase with Leo it was when he went to the other woman to both trigger me to get his supply and to get me to chase him. When he came back to me I felt like I had "won," but ultimately every time I went back I was the one that was losing. The end of the cycle and final discard only happened when I made the choice to have very minimal contact with him and eventually no contact. Ideally the way to get out of the cycle is no contact completely. The only reason not to go no contact is if you have children together. This is when you need to have as minimal contact as possible.

> **#LOVEBOMB: THE GRAY ROCK METHOD**
>
> There is a method called the "Gray Rock Method" for those who have children with narcissists or have them as family members. This is essentially about remaining as unemotionally responsive as possible to the narcissists poking and prodding. Basically you act as boring as a gray rock. This way they are not able to get the same supply from you if you do react to them and will turn more of their energy to somewhere they can get the attention they need.

Other than that, cut your losses and run! I got to a point where I stopped caring about the threats of what he would do to me if I left him. I knew that nothing would ever be as bad as staying in that toxicity.

And then you will have your FREEDOMMMM BABY!

Owning Your Inner Narcissist

I remember sitting in a Spiral Clearing Workshop one day ran by Dane Tomas and he said something like "one of the reasons why empaths attract narcissists is because they haven't owned their own inner narcissist, this energy is suppressed in them."

When he said these words I could feel the truth of that in my body. That stuck out for me the most at that workshop and it wasn't even about narcissism or empaths!

Had I been judging narcissistic behaviour?

Had I been so afraid to appear narcissistic that I was attracting it until I learned how to own and love this part of myself?

Possibly ... yes!

As the saying goes: "what you resist persists". The more I avoided and judged my own narcissistic traits, the more I was attracting it until I owned and loved this in myself.

It sounds odd, but in order to heal my self-love deficit disorder and stop attracting narcissists, I had to love and own my inner narcissist!

When I read the behaviours of the narcissists I could see that I had some of these traits too!

I sometimes questioned whether it was me that was the narcissist! Because I also liked getting attention and being noticed by people, I too had lied to get what I wanted and needed in the past, I too had been jealous and controlling at times, I too sought approval from others, I too had my ego boosted when people gave me praise and adoration, I too have projected my feelings onto others … the list could go on here!

If I was judging these traits in them that were in me, it meant I was judging them in myself and the only way for them to stop showing up in my life meant that I had to look at these, own and integrate them, and then choose to show up differently. My willingness to do this meant I wasn't a narcissist, because a narcissist wouldn't be willing to truly own their behaviour and change it.

That coupled with the fact that I do genuinely feel empathy and compassion for others means that I am not an actual narcissist!

The truth is that every person on this planet has some narcissistic traits and behaviours. We live in a world where we are conditioned that we need to get love and approval from others to belong and to survive. We are not really taught that this love and approval can actually come from inside of us.

The first step to this is to reclaim your lovebombing for yourself. This means lovebombing the shit out of yourself!

#LOVEPRACTICE: OWNING YOUR INNER NARCISSIST

The opportunity here now is to own the narcissistic traits you may have. Have a look at the lists above and identify the behaviours that you have done or currently do. It's not about trying to necessarily change them, it's about owning the trait by asking yourself:

1. What are the behaviours and traits I need to own?
2. Am I willing to learn how to love this part of me?
3. How has this behaviour actually been serving me?
4. What needs was I trying to get met by acting this way?

Write the answers to these questions below

Lovebombing the Shit Out of Yourself

You will have noticed that I use the word '#LOVEBOMB' in this book, this is because I want you to reclaim this for yourself!

So are you willing to behave like a narcissist? I don't mean going out and deliberately manipulating people for your own gain. What I mean is:

- Are you willing to truly love yourself?
- Are you willing to be selfish and put yourself first?
- Are you willing to completely and utterly adore yourself?
- Are you willing to share your achievements with others?
- Are you willing to be super proud of yourself?

These are all ways of behaving that have often been made wrong and bad by society. We are conditioned that loving ourselves and sharing about our successes is selfish or "up ourselves." But when this behaviour comes from a healthy place (and not to hurt, prove ourselves, to or manipulate others), it then stops us from seeking love and approval from outside of ourselves. This way you are much less likely to be co-dependent and you can authentically give love to others from the overflow of your own love cup rather than from a half-full or empty place.

Write out 5 ways below that you can lovebomb yourself on a daily basis.

1.
2.
3.
4.
5.

So the medicine to stop attracting narcissists is in fact to lovebomb the shit out of yourself and then to catch yourself when you are devaluing yourself and discarding yourself!

Can you now see that the narcissist was reflecting the ways you devalue and abandon yourself?

When you value yourself and set healthy boundaries around your time and energy, you won't be giving the narcissist enough supply to stay interested in pursuing you!

Owning Judgement as a Pathway to Self-Love

Let me be very clear here that none of this excuses the narcissist's behaviour and it is also not okay to stay in a relationship with a narcissist because you think they are there to show you what you need to love and own in you!

After I went through the process of owning my inner narcissist, my energy on narcissism changed and I actually stopped being attracted to narcissists. But it was only after exiting the relationship that I was able to truly self-reflect and embody what I needed to learn from being in the relationship with them.

If you notice yourself judging someone and their behaviour, ask yourself "how can I bring this into love?" and then use the questions in the above exercise to see what is wanting to be seen, owned and integrated inside of you.

Every judgement on another is simply showing you how you can love yourself more.

We can also recognise that there is a difference between a human being and their behaviour. Can you see that they are simply a human trying to get needs met and that they are most often just acting from past trauma and pain?

This doesn't mean that you have to hang out with that person or be friends with them either. Please understand that not everyone will approve of you and if they don't like you it actually doesn't make you any less lovable!

I always say "you can have compassion, but with healthy boundaries!".

Chapter 14
Emotional Unavailability and Ghosting

"One day I realised that it was me who was the emotionally unavailable one all along"

Ahhhh yes! The infamous disappearing act now coined as – Ghosting!

Whenever I wasn't being lovebombed by narcissists I found myself attracting men who were never quite available to me.

Everything would seemingly be going great and then out of nowhere the person would withdraw their energy or just disappear, without a trace and no explanation as to why. It would be highly confusing, devastating, and soul-crushing for me. This would send me into a spiral of self-doubt and constant questioning thoughts which drove me into loony town and further into feeling I needed to change or prove myself to them.

These were also the same feelings that happened when I was in the discard phase of the narcissist.

The worst part was just simply the not knowing and the constant wondering where I went wrong!

Wishing that they would at least tell me something … anything! Pleeeeease!

And then more silence …

Become The One

And more devastation and confusion ...

And the constant monkey mind thoughts that went from blaming myself for fucking it all up to blaming him for being such a stubborn, ignorant asshole!

I would either text and call these men trying to find out what happened or try to play it cool whilst internalising it and numbing the feelings of rejection.

I would be telling myself a bunch of stories about why I'm not good enough whilst my abandonment wounds were triggered as fuck. I would give my power away trying to win them back and prove myself to them to show them why they should still want me!

The very act of trying to get their attention would only tend to push them away even more.

I would often wonder "why am I acting like this crazy person? Who have I become?!"

If I eventually heard from the men they would say things like "I'm not ready for a relationship" or "I can only be friends right now" or "it's not the right time" or "I've met someone else."

Either that or I would find out they already had a girlfriend, were still involved with their ex, or recently broke up with their ex and were not available emotionally.

But some of them would even just seemingly drop off the face of the earth, never to be seen or heard from again!

Many of these men were the very same ones I was trying to rescue too. Their broken hearts kicked my rescuer right into action and then the very act of trying to rescue someone who doesn't want to be rescued would push them away.

After all I had done to help them, how could they just ignore me like that?

Emotional Unavailability and Ghosting

And ***POOF*** – just like that they were gone.

> **#LOVEBOMB: GHOSTERS DID YOU A FAVOUR**
>
> When someone ghosts you it doesn't mean that you are rejected, it really means that they are not in alignment with your values and what you want and they, in fact, actually did you a favour!
>
> Every person who magically disappears from your life is actually giving you a gift and that gift is to help you to show up in more love and presence with yourself. They also create more space for someone who is available!
>
> **When you get triggered by being ghosted ask yourself:**
>
> - Where are you ignoring yourself and your needs?
> - Where are you not being available?
>
> **Then hold space for yourself** by naming and feeling your triggered emotions and meeting your needs daily. Remember to use the trigger healing practice! This is how YOU become more emotionally available and hence attract someone who is more emotionally available too.

So I wondered why this kept happening to me? What the fuck was I doing so wrong to deserve being treated like this?

One of my biggest triggers was when I was being ignored by someone. My ex-husband in particular would ignore me for days on end without any explanation and I would create all sorts of painful stories in my mind about what he was doing and how he didn't love or care about me.

I was so desperate to change these stories that I set out on a mission to find out why this kept happening to me! That's when I eventually discovered that one of the reasons was because I was trying to "win" unavailable men over to prove that I was wanted. This stemmed back to my childhood to the times when my dad wasn't emotionally available or fully present for me and when he was physically away for three years when my parents separated.

I had been trying to unconsciously heal this childhood wound by trying to win over each man. But instead I just kept validating the belief I had that "I am not wanted" and playing out my abandonment and rejection wounds.

This is why when someone pulled away or ghosted me it made me go into such emotional turmoil and desperation. I felt abandoned.

#LOVEBOMB: WHY MEN REALLY PULL AWAY

Men pull away for many different reasons, they also have their own fears and triggers that come up that have nothing to do with us. One of my past co-facilitators, Dating Coach, Mark Rosenfeld has some insightful videos on YouTube on why men really pull away, they are definitely worth a watch!

One of the reasons a healthy man pulls away after he seems really interested in you is often because he actually likes you and he needs to take time to decide whether he is willing to give up some of his freedom to be with you. If in that time you text and call constantly it will often make him think that he will lose his freedom and he may then go into resistance and want to avoid you!

I know sometimes this is hard to do, especially if you really like the guy and you want to know how he feels about you, but this is the time where you must be incredibly patient and wait for him to come to you. This is when you need to show up as your own parent, to show up with your own masculine presence. You have to give yourself the loving presence and emotional support for the times you didn't get that as a child.

If he doesn't come back, then he wasn't truly available for you anyway and he ultimately did you a favour!

Emotional Unavailability and Ghosting

I Was the Emotionally Unavailable One

The biggest "AHA" for me around attracting what I thought were "emotionally unavailable men" was discovering that it was actually me who was emotionally unavailable!

For years I thought I was just so open to love. I deeply longed for it. I thought I wore my heart on my sleeve and always gave so much of myself in relationships.

But when I was ignored and felt rejected I wasn't giving myself that loving presence or emotional support that I wanted from them; I was instead numbing the painful emotions.

Whilst I was numbing any kind of feeling my heart was never going to be open to receiving someone else's love.

How could I receive their love, when I wasn't even receiving my own?

Here I was, pointing my finger at these men and thinking to myself "if only he stopped being so afraid, he would open his heart and he could feel the love that was possible with us!"

But what I really had to do was turn that finger around and say to myself "if only I stopped being so afraid, I would open my own heart and I would see what was possible to love within myself!"

Write below some of the things that you have wished men would have done for you:

_____
_____
_____
_____
_____
_____

Now flip that around now and say it to yourself as I did above:

Interesting isn't it?

Even though I thought my heart was open, I really had no idea how closed it actually was.

> **#LOVETIP: DOING THE WORK TO TURN IT AROUND**
>
> In Byron Katie's "the work" she teaches a powerful turn around process to flip around any complaint or thought you have about someone, as below:
>
> 1. What is the complaint/should?
> 2. Do I know that this is completely and absolutely true?
> 3. How do I act/treat them when I think this thought?
> 4. How does it feel to be this way?
> 5. Who would you be if you didn't believe this?
> 6. Turn it around on yourself (swap the 'them/he/she/their name' for 'I/myself/my name')
>
> Give it a try now!

I Had A Giant "Fuck Off" Wall Around My Heart

All the years of abuse. All the years of numbing my pain. All the years of searching for love outside of myself and never quite finding it. All the years of feeling rejected and unwanted.

This had led me to creating that giant, energetic "fuck off" wall around my heart. I was unconsciously pushing men away by self-sabotaging the connection and then I was blaming them for not being available!

I wanted so desperately to fall in love and have a happy, healthy relationship, but no matter what I did I would either choose someone unhealthy or someone who wasn't available.

What I came to learn was that I was choosing unavailable men because they were safe. What I mean by this is that my brain was choosing unavailable men because that was what was familiar. My brain was also trying to protect me from falling in love and getting my heart broken again.

Because how could I fall in love with someone if they weren't available to be with?

At times I thought I may have been in love with them, but it was only the "love drugs" that were heightened when I was with them and lowered when they disappeared. My heart still felt broken at times, but I would quickly numb that pain and move onto the next person and I would close my heart just that little bit more each time, which only made me more unavailable!

I Chose Unavailable Men to Avoid Being Vulnerable

It was safer this way because I would never end up having a relationship with them and they would never get to see underneath my confident, happy facade, because what was underneath my "fuck off" wall was a whole lot of vulnerability—the deep grief of feeling worthless.

I soon realised that all these men were simply a reflection of my self-rejection, self-abandonment, and my own emotional unavailability. They were there mirroring my own closed heart.

You attract unavailable people because there are parts of yourself that are unavailable. You know the parts I am talking about, the super scary, edgy vulnerable ones that you do anything to avoid them being seen!

So when you lean into your vulnerability and start allowing those places that you hide to be seen by others, you start to become more available and so do the people around you!

Behaviours of Being Unavailable

- Choosing and attracting people who are essentially unavailable whether that be that they are with someone else, they are not ready for a relationship, or they are not emotionally available.
- Had a parent or caregiver who was often not present or available or not around at all.
- You are trying to win over that person as a way to unconsciously heal your childhood wounds.
- People pull away or run away from you which triggers your abandonment wounds.
- You react to people pulling away by numbing your feelings or cutting the other person off to try and regain power and control.
- You regret cutting people off and try and win them back by convincing or proving yourself to them.
- The other person's avoidance and distance tends to validate your abandonment and rejection wounds.
- You are actually unconsciously keeping yourself safe from ever getting too close to them to avoid being hurt or being seen in your vulnerabilities.

#LOVEPRACTICE: OWNING YOUR UNAVAILABILITY

Write out the ways that you have been unavailable. Identify why you have attracted unavailable people.

Chapter 15

The Self-Sabotager and Friendzoner

"It looked like they were the one leaving me, when really I pushed them away"

Have you done quite a bit of the old self-sabotage?

*I have! I have! I have! *throws hands in the air**

We have so much fear when it comes to having a loving relationship, that sometimes we will unconsciously push away the very thing that we are deeply yearning for.

As I said earlier, I longed for a healthy, happy relationship. But what did I do when I met a healthy, available man?

I completely sabotaged it!

I would be interested, but pretend not to be interested.

God forbid they find out I liked them, that would be the end of the world as I know it, I could get rejected and that would just be way too painful and embarrassing!

So I put them on a pedestal and decided they were far too good for me, and that they could never possibly like me back! I would be forever looking up to them and devaluing myself at the same time.

Putting Men in the Friendzone

The safest thing for me to do was to friendzone them of course! I would try and find reasons not to be interested in them romantically and tried to focus on for their flaws. I often turned them into business colleagues and told myself we could never possibly date!

I would then try to prove myself to them through overgiving and running my caretaker role.

I was secretly hoping that they would like me and see how amazing I am by all the things I am giving them and how much we had in common. I would be waiting for them to make the first move of course, which usually never happened since I showed very little romantic interest in them at all as we hung out in the friendzone! My masculine was "bro-ing" out with their masculine and there was no room for polarity (aka attraction)! But of course, this was the energy I had gone into to feel safe.

If I found out they liked or were dating someone else and they proceeded to tell me about the other person and how awesome they were, I would get upset and frustratingly wonder. What about me and my awesomeness? Couldn't they see that?

No, they couldn't see that because I had stopped being myself and I had started moulding myself into someone I thought they would like. I had also shut down my sexy, sensual playful side, because we were "just friends", which made them only see me only as a friend!

Checking Out at the First Sign of Rejection

How about the "I'll reject you before you reject me card".

Now let's say a man I liked did express interest in me and we started dating. If there was any sign that they might reject me or that they might not like me as much as I liked them or there was any kind of

The Self-Sabotager and Friendzoner

conflict I automatically pulled my energy away and put my "fuck off" wall up.

I would distance myself or put them back into the friendzone—"we are just better off as friends" which really meant "I'm scared you are going to reject me and leave me and this feels safer."

This was me checking out of the connection before my feelings got too involved.

Underneath this behaviour I was running stories such as "I'm not worthy of this person/their love," "I'll get rejected," "they will leave me," "they are too good for me," "I don't deserve this."

I was so afraid to be seen by them that it was easier for me to check out when I thought they may see that I am not good enough for them. But by me energetically pulling away and checking out, this would give them a signal to leave and often it then looked like they were the one leaving me when I was really the one that left.

Then I got to prove the belief "they will leave me" to be true, even though it was me that energetically left first!

> **#LOVEBOMB: PULLING AWAY TO PROTECT YOURSELF**
>
> Protecting your heart ultimately backfires on you. Your unavailability ends up hurting you when you unconsciously push others away and self-sabotage. It may look like they left you, but ultimately you will have pulled away or checked out first. Then you are getting to prove the beliefs such as "I always get rejected, people always leave me".

Behaviours of the Self-Sabotager

- Friendzoning to keep yourself safe when if you were really honest you are actually interested in them as more than a friend
- Pedestalling them and devaluing yourself

- Looking for their flaws and reasons not to be attracted to them
- Hiding your feelings and pretending not to like them because you are afraid if they found out you would be rejected
- Making up and telling yourself stories as to why it won't work with them
- Telling yourself stories about why you aren't good enough for them or the relationship and using this as a reason to distance yourself
- Pulling away or emotionally checking out at the first sign they may reject or leave you
- Playing the "I'll reject you before you reject me" protection card

#LOVEPRACTICE: OWNING YOUR SELF-SABOTAGER

Write out how you can see how you have self-sabotaged your relationships.

_____
_____
_____
_____
_____
_____
_____
_____
_____
_____
_____
_____

Chapter 16
The Non-Committed Push-Puller

"It is only from a strong foundation of safety that a relationship can flourish and grow into a healthy long-term commitment."

I want you, I don't want you, I want you, I don't want you ...

This is extremely confusing and sometimes can be a volatile push/pull, hot/cold, on/off effect!

I was consistently keeping one foot out the door in my relationships "just in case it doesn't work out", I never allowed my heart to fully be in them.

This created a lack of safety for both myself and the other person.

How could I expect the other person to commit and give themselves fully to the relationship when I wasn't willing to do the same?

This was also a dynamic that played out in my childhood. My Dad once shared with me that when I was a child sometimes he wanted me around and sometimes he didn't and energetically I would have picked up on that. Again, it's not my Dad's fault and I am sure my Mum experienced these same feelings too. I think almost every parent experiences these feelings due to their own stress and emotional state, sometimes they love having their kids around and other times they wish they could ship them off somewhere for a little while!

You Are Either 100% or You Are 100% Out

Safety is foundational to having a healthy relationship.

You can't have safety in a relationship when one or both people have one foot out the door.

If you show up only half in, this energetically signals the other person that you may leave and then they may check out and then they may also have one foot out the door!

Neither of you then feels secure in the relationship. This can lead to one or both people trying to control the person or the relationship or other person.

This showed up with Leo, to the point where we were living together and he never unpacked his suitcase just in case he had to leave or I kicked him out for the 17th time (in his words)! You can imagine that it didn't make either of us feel very secure.

From the moment when he first discarded me I had actually emotionally checked out, which was less than a month into our relationship! From that moment on neither of us was 100% in there.

I said to him at one point "I want to check back in, I want to feel safe enough to be in love with you."

But no matter how much I tried it was never going to happen because he was not a safe man and I always felt on edge with him. The more that I got triggered by him the less safe I felt. I just checked out and shut down which led to more triggering and less safety!

This became a cycle that created a push/pull effect. We were then both trying to control each other and the relationship in different ways because neither of us felt safe. It was a constant power struggle!

Checking Back in With Yourself

I knew I had to take time out for myself to heal so that I could create emotional safety within myself first. The person I really needed to be back in love with was me!

To create emotional safety in a relationship you need to have boundaries and agreements and be able to speak openly about your vulnerabilities. You also need to have agreements to not threaten to leave each other in the heat of a conflict. No big decisions should ever be made whilst in a triggered state.

If that person is not willing to hear you and make agreements to honour each other's boundaries, then it's going to be very hard to feel safe in that relationship. It is only from a foundation of safety that a relationship can flourish and grow into a long-term commitment. You have to create safety inside of you first by having your own healthy boundaries and commitments to yourself, as well as creating the space and time to feel your emotions.

#LOVEBOMB: ARE YOU NON-COMMITTAL?

If someone appears to be "non-committal" or you are the one being non-committal, ask yourself:

- Where am I not fully committing in my life?
- Where am I not committing to myself?
- Where am I not committing to the another person fully? Why is that? Is there something I am afraid of or somewhere I don't feel safe? Is there a boundary or agreement I need to feel safe?

"How Do You Have a Relationship and Not Lose Yourself?"

This is one of the most common questions I get asked by my clients and the reason for this is because so many people have lost themselves in their relationships which comes from having a lack of boundaries and getting caught up in the happy chemical highs at the start of the relationship. People start giving up their own interests to spend time with the other person and over time they lose sight of themselves as they are not meeting their own values as they did when they were single.

My clients tell me they are hesitant to go all in for a relationship again or to fully commit to someone because they are afraid they will lose something, usually themselves, their freedom or their purpose!

There seems to be a disempowering belief that when you commit to someone you are having to give up or sacrifice something you want or love. But think about what is possible if you could be in relationship that supports your current life rather than takes away from it!

Can You Have a Successful Career and a Healthy Relationship?

It may be hard to believe that this is even possible if you have never experienced it or have not seen it modelled to you. With my clients who are extremely successful career women I notice that they have had a disempowering belief that they can't have both a relationship and a successful career; that it is either one or the other, but not both. The most common way I see women losing themselves very quickly is when they are running the role of people pleaser.

This is for many reasons, but also because it's in a woman's instinctual nature to please a man so that he will protect her. So she will often go into unconsciously pleasing a man.

The Non-Committed Push-Puller

This is why having an awareness of your patterns and having a healthy, solid relationship with yourself first is vital before entering into a serious committed relationship. You can then recognise and call yourself on it when you see yourself going into pleasing or sacrificing your own wants and needs.

Treat yourself as you would a partner by committing to yourself daily and growing deeper into your own love. The key here is that you must maintain this with yourself even when you are in a relationship with another. Without commitment to yourself first, you can never fully commit to another person or expect to receive the same level of commitment from them.

It's about being your own fully committed parent to your inner child, being fully there to self-soothe and love them especially in those more vulnerable moments where you might want to check out.

It's about having healthy boundaries that make you feel safe to be vulnerable and open - having your inner masculine support your inner feminine.

#LOVEBOMB: GETTING YOURSELF BACK

Always maintain your own interests, take things slowly at the start and set healthy boundaries around how much time you spend together. Don't give up spending time with your friends and on your hobbies to spend time with them. Ultimately you shouldn't be giving up the things that help you live inside of your values just because you are in a relationship.

The extra bonus is that this also creates more sexual chemistry and attraction! If you are in a relationship write a list of what you have given up since being in the relationship. Make a commitment to add the things on the list that brought you the most joy on your own. You actually only need to have 25% values in common to have a successful relationship.

Behaviours of the Non-Committed Push-Puller

- Have lost yourself in previous relationships and are afraid it will happen again.
- Drop your own interests to please or spend time with the other person.
- Have one foot out the door just in case it doesn't work out.
- Feel a push / pull, repulsion / attraction energy towards the other person; sometimes you want them and other times you don't.
- Often don't feel safe in the relationship or in the world.
- Don't feel safe inside your body and find yourself in your head a lot.
- Not in touch with your own emotions and often feel numb.
- Have a fear of commitment because you believe that commitment means a loss of freedom or that there is some other kind of sacrifice you will have to make
- Do not believe you can have both a relationship and a successful career.

#LOVEPRACTICE: OWN YOUR NON-COMMITTAL PUSH-PULLER

Write out the ways that you haven't been committed to yourself and others and how you have pushed and pulled.

_____
_____
_____
_____
_____
_____

Chapter 17
The Avoidant Settler

"Settling to avoid experiencing your deeper fears is where you betray yourself and your birthright to have epic love"

You know those people who seem to jump from one relationship to the next? You may even be one of them!

Or the ones who just seem to settle for what's in front of them or whoever shows up next in their space that shows them a bit of interest?

They stay in a relationship that isn't going to grow, that may even know that person isn't quite right for them.

Perhaps it's because they believe that's the best that they can get or deserve?

Or they are jumping into another connection to avoid feeling the pain from the last break-up.

Maybe it's because they are deeply afraid to be alone and need someone around to feel some kind of security or validation.

Now, I've been single a lot in my life, but I have settled before too. I've chosen to be with men who I knew were not right for me. I had such a lack of self-worth and fear of being alone that I just went with it or stayed in it.

I was often with men who loved me more than I loved them and so it seemed very safe for me to be with them because they were less likely to leave me.

I told myself that one day I would fall in love with them too.

As time went on I hoped my love for them would grow, but that day never came. Of course this never ended well, because just like the push-puller, I was never 100% checked in and I usually ended up pushing them away!

> **#LOVETIP: THE AVOIDANT AND THE ANXIOUS**
>
> In Stan Tatkin's book *Wired for Love* he shares about different attachment styles - the avoidant, the anxious and the secure.
>
> In the last chapter and this chapter I am covering a lot of the behaviours of the avoidant attachment style.
>
> Someone who is more anxious will often be attracted to someone who is more avoidant and they play out the push/pull dynamics.
>
> Essentially the anxious feels safer around people and the avoidant feels safer on their own. Both have a fear of abandonment - being abandoned and losing themselves respectively.
>
> Ultimately what needs to happen is for both people to come into a more secure attachment style to create safety in that relationship.
>
> I've seen myself go between the two styles based on the person I am with and where I am at emotionally. Doing this work has really helped me come into more of a secure attachment style.
>
> To download a copy of the attachment styles quiz and find out your style go to www.ejlove.com/attachmentstylesquiz.

The Avoidant Settler

Choosing What You Think Is Safe

Two commonalities I see with women who have experienced abuse is that they either choose someone to repeat the abusive pattern with or they settle with someone they do not feel a deep emotional connection with or attraction to, because they are trying to keep themselves safe from experiencing the abuse again.

It's natural that after you have experienced something toxic or abusive you would be afraid to experience that again. But when you settle you actually may be avoiding dealing with healing from the pain of that toxic experience.

This is where you may choose the "nice guy" or the pushover or the "good girl" or the doormat, because underneath you know they would be less likely to leave you and you will have some control and safety in the relationship. This is just another form of co-dependency.

As one of my as one of my mentors, Alex Tripod, would say 'that relationship is a 7 out of 10'!

You know you are not truly in love with them. You stay in it hoping that one day something will change. But the spark and deep love and connection just isn't quite ever there.

So here you are choosing people where you are less likely to go all in with emotionally so you won't be as vulnerable with them or truly open your heart, and there is far less risk of them hurting you ... *or so you think*.

I still had my share of heartbreaks from men I "settled" with. It was never as intense as the hurt from the narcissists, but it still hurt!

The Fear of Being Alone and the Fear of Intimacy

What can be sitting underneath your choice to be or stay with someone who you know isn't right for you is a fear of being alone. This is why it's so important to spend time on your own even when you are in a relationship.

The other fear that sits there is the fear of intimacy. I'm not talking about sex here. I'm talking about being seen in your vulnerabilities, being seen in the parts of yourself that you may feel most insecure about or aren't lovable or good enough.

It's allowing all of that to be seen by someone you deeply love and that feels so risky. Because there is a risk that if they see all of you, they may not like all of you or want to be with you anymore, and then they may abandon you, or hurt you deeply in some way.

It's also a whole lot less emotionally riskier if you spend time with people who you don't share yourself with fully or someone that you are not really all that into!

> **#LOVETIP: THE FEAR OF INTIMACY**
>
> In the book *Are you the One for Me* by Barbara De Angelis she says that it is not the fear of intimacy that we are afraid of, it's the fear of the consequences of intimacy.
>
> If you associate intimacy with abandonment, abuse, rejection, criticism or any another form of pain, ultimately you will be unconsciously avoiding intimacy even though it's what you deeply crave. The more you are willing to be vulnerable and heal the source of pain you have associated intimacy with, the more you will be open to experiencing the level of intimacy you truly desire!

People may believe that they are the one with more power if they are less emotionally invested, but the truth is the person who has the most power is the one who is willing to be vulnerable and feel everything!

The reality is that when you are avoiding something, you are the one who is giving your power away.

Using Casual Dating and Sex to Avoid True Intimacy

Casual dating and sex can be A LOT of fun and as you now know I've had my fair share of this in my life!

So my question to people now who tend to do this a lot is, "are you dating a lot of different people and having sex to avoid deep emotional connection and being vulnerable? You know sharing all the scary stuff!"

One of the ways you can avoid intimacy is by settling for something that isn't what you truly want, like just having casual sex all the time when what you really want is a deeply loving relationship.

Perhaps you keep dating people who are definitely not people you would want to be in a relationship with. You may say things like they are "just a bit of fun" for now. They are just "Mr or Mrs Right Now", they are a "you'll do"!

Now I do encourage you to get your needs met through exploring different connections, but I want you to also be aware of when it may be coming from avoidance and completely outsourcing your needs or when it is coming from a genuine curiosity to explore the different parts of yourself these people activate in you from a place of your own fullness.

In shadow, you may have had lots of one-night stands or used sex as a way to get love, validation, and approval. Yet, so often you have felt empty afterwards.

Underneath that is a longing for something much deeper. But you still keep choosing people who are not going to give you that and then get frustrated on why you can never seem to be able to attract the kind of person who wants that.

Avoidance and the Fear of Abandonment

If you find yourself attracting people who are avoidant or you are continuing to settle time and time again, but you still find yourself longing for something more, you have to ask yourself—what am I REALLY avoiding here?

Usually you will find it is some kind of vulnerability that you are afraid will be seen that is unconsciously creating this avoidance. You may be attracting others who may be avoidant as well to keep you safe from having to share this part of yourself (or they may trigger the fuck out of it!)

My recommendation is to begin sharing the parts of yourself you feel vulnerable about with your friends who you feel safe to share with. Join women's circles or men's groups where you can safely express these parts of yourself. There are also circles inclusive of all genders and non-binary.

#LOVETIP: EXPRESSING YOUR VULNERABILITIES

Harness some courage and share with your lovers, friends and partners the things that make you feel vulnerable, the things that you are afraid to share the most!

You can begin with:

'Can I share something with you that feels really vulnerable for me?'

'It feels vulnerable to share this with you…'

'This is what makes me feel most vulnerable…'

'What I have been avoiding sharing with you is…'

In the notes section in the back of this book write down the things

> that you feel most vulnerable for you to share and then ask someone close to you to have a conversation to share these with them. Give them an opportunity to also share what is most vulnerable for them too.
>
> No matter what the outcome of their response - acknowledge yourself for simple taking action - this is your gateway to true intimacy.

Behaviours of the Avoidant Settler

- Chosen to be with people who you know weren't quite right for you.
- Have been with people who tend to be more emotionally invested in you than you are with them.
- Stayed in a relationship for much longer than you know you should have.
- Have a deep fear of being alone.
- Jumped from relationship to relationship without having much time to heal from the previous one.
- Used sex and casual dating to numb your feelings or avoid emotional connection or as a way to get love, validation, and approval.
- Have a fear of intimacy and being truly seen by others, especially your perceived flaws and vulnerabilities, and you are afraid they will see that you are not good enough and will leave you or hurt you in some way.
- Avoid being emotionally vulnerable and sharing what really scares you.

#LOVEPRACTICE: OWNING YOUR AVOIDANT SETTLER

Write out the ways that you have avoided and settled for less than what you truly desire in love.

_____
_____
_____
_____
_____
_____
_____
_____
_____
_____
_____
_____
_____
_____
_____
_____
_____
_____
_____
_____
_____
_____
_____
_____
_____

Chapter 18

Reclaim Your Power in Love

"Your true power lies in your willingness to look in the mirror"

I am imagining that you have had a series of lightbulbs go off and you may be thinking *well, that's great, EJ, but how the hell do I now stop these patterns from happening again?*

Why, I'm so glad you asked!

Because now you simply get to **CHOOSE DIFFERENTLY**.

It sounds a lot easier than it is, I know!

You see you didn't know what you didn't know, but now you do know - got it?

By reading this far you have begun to make the unconscious conscious, and this is the first step into being able to choose differently next time.

I have broken this into a seven-step process to help you do this with ease.

The way that we reclaim our power is by deep self-reflection on all the ways we have, most often unconsciously, given our power away. When we can sit back and truly see the roles, behaviours and patterns we have played out and fully own our part in it, this is where our true power lies.

The following seven-step power reclamation process that I am about to guide you through will help you step out of your old, unhealthy ways of relating and into an empowered way of relating:

The Power Reclamation Process
1. Owning your Behaviour
2. Looking in the Mirror
3. Self-forgiveness Ritual
4. Identifying your Disempowering Stories
5. Discovering your Empowered Truth
6. Showing Up in your Soul-aligned Truth
7. Making a Commitment to Self

In this chapter I will be taking you through the first four steps which are focused on identifying and letting go of these old, disempowered ways of showing up. In the next chapter you will learn how to show up as your real, raw, completely lovable, worthy self!

When you let go of what doesn't serve you, you make room for what does.

STEP 1: Owning Your Behaviour

Reflecting on your answers from the previous chapters on patterns, write out how you can see that you have given your power away in your relationships.

What behaviours do you have to own here to reclaim your power?

Refer to the previous chapters **on patterns** *ie enabling abuse, being a rescuer, overgiving, martyring myself, people pleasing, not having healthy boundaries, not listening to your intuition, self-sabotaging.*

STEP 2: Looking in the Mirror

It's time to take a long, hard look in the mirror at yourself! Not an actual mirror, but seeing the mirror of their behaviour that has shown up in you too.

Often we will project onto others the unowned parts of ourselves.

Your relationships are also reflective of the relationship you have with yourself and people will generally show up and treat you in ways that are reflective of how you treat yourself.

So for example if someone is abusing you or betraying you, the question to ask is "how have I been abusing and betraying myself?"

With Leo, the way that I was abusing and betraying myself was actually by staying in an abusive relationship. How could I expect him to honour me when I wasn't honouring myself by staying in a relationship that was hurting me so deeply?

Relationship Mirrors are Our Greatest Teachers

When you start showing up loving, honouring, respecting, and valuing yourself, I can guarantee you that the people who show up will reflect this back to you. You teach others how to treat you by what you allow and set boundaries for.

The other piece of self-responsibility is to look at where you also have done or have been doing the same thing as that person, whether it be with them, or with someone else. The mirror may be that you have been judging that person and it is showing you that this judgement needs to be seen and brought into love. We all hold something we judge in another within us too to a degree, so whatever you judge in another is seeking to be loved in you.

When I did the self-responsibility process around Leo I could see the ways that I had also hurt him and I had to really own those. It wasn't safe for me to speak to him directly to own my part in it, so I did this instead in a just as powerful soul-to-soul completion conversation which I will take you through in the next chapter.

> **#LOVEBOMB: SELF-COMPASSION FOR JUDGEMENTS**
>
> Can you love the part of you that judges others?
>
> Can you love the part of you that judges yourself?
>
> As Matt Kahn says, when you judge others, you are withdrawing love from yourself.
>
> Have compassion for the part of you that judges and then ask yourself:
>
> *How you can I see this judgement through the eyes of love?*
>
> *What is it here to teach me?*
>
> *What is wanting to be owned and brought into love?*

#LOVEPRACTICE: MIRROR JOURNALLING

Reflect back to the exercise in chapter 5 when you told your story from the victimised perspective and write out the answers in the notes page of the back of this book to the following questions:

- Where was I doing the same or similar thing?
- What can I now take self-responsibility for?
- How does this mirror the way I treat myself?
- What have I been judging the other person for?
- How is this reflective of where I judge myself?
- What can I now see are the parts of myself that are seeking to be seen and loved?

STEP 3: Self-Forgiveness Ritual

I grew up hearing the saying "forgive and forget," except I didn't know what forgiveness really meant and my "forgetting" experience actually was more along the lines of "move on by numbing the pain." I always thought forgiveness meant forgiving another person, but what's most important is forgiving ourselves.

So what if I told you that you didn't actually have to forgive anyone if you didn't want to? That in fact, the only person you really need to forgive is yourself. Forgiving others isn't really about them, it's about giving your own soul peace. The real forgiveness towards them comes when you see the gift in the experience and then there is really nothing to forgive.

Forgive Yourself to Surrender to Love

A psychic once said to me that "the only way you are going to fall in love again is if you forgive yourself. You have to let go of control through forgiveness."

She was right because love is something we surrender to, not something we can control. You will only allow yourself to open to a deep love when you feel safe to surrender to it. When your heart feels held and safe it will let go into love.

At that time, I was running stories that it wasn't safe for me to love or to even be loved; hence, well, I tried to control everything!

In this step you are forgiving yourself for showing up in a way that didn't honour you. You are going to do this through a self-forgiveness ritual.

In *The Book of Forgiving* by Desmond Tutu and Mpho Tutu they offer a "Hand of Mercy Ritual" where they propose that our left hand is the hand of judgement and our right hand is the hand of mercy and forgiveness. I am adapting from this and doing a similar ritual.

> **#LOVEGIFT: SELF-FORGIVENESS RITUAL**
>
> Head on over to www.ejlove.com/forgivenessritual where you will get immediate access to my video that takes you through the ritual below and you will also receive a suggested list of all the behaviours and patterns you may want to forgive yourself for.

What are you choosing to forgive yourself for?

Start by writing out the answers to the following questions by reflecting back to the previous steps and seeing all the ways you showed up in your old patterns, in your old story, and all the things you are taking responsibility for now. These are what you are forgiving yourself for and anything else you may like to add here.

#LOVEPRACTICE: THE HAND OF MERCY RITUAL

You will need: A mirror and a stone or crystal

1. Put stone in your left hand and say "I forgive myself for ..." whilst looking into your left eye in the mirror.
2. Then bring the stone to the heart, breathe in the feeling of love and compassion, and then place the stone in your right hand.
3. Go through and do this for each forgiveness statement until you are complete.
4. Hold both hands to your heart, close your eyes, take a deep breath in, and say "I love myself and I deeply honour my humanness."

Forgiving Yourself With the Ho'oponopono Prayer

A powerful practice to forgive yourself is through the Ho'oponopono prayer. This is a very powerful practice to do with your inner child. The prayer is a well-known Hawaiian prayer created by Hawaiian therapist Dr Ihaleakala Hew Len. It consists of four elements: repentance, forgiveness, gratitude, and love.

These are the four words:-
1. I'm sorry
2. Please forgive me
3. Thank you
4. I love you

I want you to go into a visualisation now and I suggest to put a timer on for five to ten minutes. You will bring forth your younger self. See them in your mind's eye standing before you. Look directly into their eyes and say "I'm sorry, please forgive me, thank you, I love you."

Keep repeating these words until the timer goes off or until you feel an energy has lifted. You may even see the energy or facial expression shift in the visualisation.

You can also use this practice anytime you feel you need to forgive someone or there is someone you need to ask forgiveness from; perhaps it may be both of you. I highly recommend to clear any resentment that you have first though by doing the emotional release work in chapter five. Otherwise you may be trying to forgive before processing the emotions, which is another form of emotional bypassing.

STEP 4: Identifying Your Disempowering Stories

As humans we love to make meaning of EVERYTHING.

You know when you receive a text from a guy and you think something like

"Ahhhh what does he mean, I wish he would just tell me!"

What if I told you that he really doesn't mean anything and he is being quite literal…yes… really!! ;)

And what if I told you that life is actually meaning-less ... it is hard for our human brain to cope with that concept ... I know!

You see, we are hardwired to find meaning. At a young age our brain is constantly searching for meaning about ourselves to make sense of who we are so that we can survive. This is when we create beliefs and stories that make up our identity.

Unfortunately, most of these stories are not true to who we actually are and are completely disempowering! But we play out these stories over and over again and relive those unhealthy relationship patterns. This is because you are functioning from an identity that isn't true to who you are as a soul.

Remember the fun you had as a child?

Running around, jumping, laughing, and playing?

You will see children often run up to another kid they have never met and just start playing and suddenly it's like they are best friends! There are no stories about whether that other kid would like them, no fear of them rejecting them or wondering if they want to talk to them or not or wondering what they think of them.

This is because most of our beliefs are formed up until the age of 21 through our parents, through society, friends, and our experiences. Usually between zero and seven years old is when we will have our first big wounding.

Sometimes this may be something traumatising like a parent that leaves or abuses you or it may be something not directly effecting you like your parents coming home with your baby brother or sister and you made it mean you weren't wanted or the chosen one anymore.

You may not even know what the experience is, as it may have been so painful that your brain has blocked it out. The emotional pain we experience in life is often not from what has happened to us, but from what we have made it mean about ourselves.

The beauty of this is that we can actually change our perspective and the meaning, and then we stop ourselves from being re-wounded.

Right, Wrong, Good, and Bad

We have be born into a society that functions on the judgements of right, wrong, and good and bad, and we most often associate "being good and right" with being worthy and lovable. We then make ourselves bad and wrong through our experiences and interactions with others based on what we have been taught is acceptable. From here we form stories about our worthiness to be loved.

I remember when I was in primary school the day I came home from school with a 97% mark on my test. I was so excited to share it with my parents. My dad was so proud of me, but my mum said to me "where is the other 3%?"

In that moment I formed a story that "no matter how well I do, it's never enough."

When I spoke to my mum about this years later, she explained to me that the reason why she asked that was because the teacher had given me ticks for everything on my test, so she was actually curious as to why the teacher hadn't marked the test as being 100%. So it wasn't even about me and how well I had or hadn't done!

She even spoke to my teacher about it and the teacher said "I never give anyone 100% even if they get everything right, because I think there is always room for improvement."

Can you imagine how damaging and confusing that was for my seven-year-old brain?

However, it's also not the teacher's fault, it is the society we live in that teaches us that there is right, wrong, good and bad, and if we somehow don't fit into it then we are somehow damaged, broken, flawed and less lovable.

Spending your Whole Life Trying to be Good Enough

Because of this meaning I created I then spent my whole life trying to achieve and do so many different things at once! I was overfunctioning with so much 'to do' and getting completely overwhelmed, jumping from one thing to the next, most often quitting projects right before they were about to become successful. Completely sabotaging myself of course!

I was always trying to prove myself by doing so much, but never quite getting to the the successful part! If I ever finished one thing, it would be straight onto the next thing I had "to do." This was costing me dearly, but I didn't know how to function any other way, it's what had become my normal - my familiar - my safe comfort zone.

I did ten things averagely instead of one thing awesomely and my personal and love life suffered. I had spent my whole life unconsciously trying to prove to my Mum that I was good enough to enough to get her love. I thought if I performed well, then I would be worthy. If it wasn't for shifting this story that I had been running, then this book would not be in your very hands!

I would have been too busy doing too many things to ever complete it, plus on top of that I had a fear of failure and success! It's somewhat a miracle that this book was completed; it took three years, a heap of internal work and hiring an awesome book writing coach to make sure it got completed and out into the world!

Trying to Prove That These Stories Are True

So you have been unconsciously spending your whole life trying to prove that all these made up meanings and stories you created when you were a child are right… how crazy is that?!

These stories are constantly being mirrored back to you in your relationships which means that you then get to prove that you are right too—"see, he never loved me," "see, I told you she would leave me," "see, I knew I wasn't good enough," "I told you that men are all liars."

Well, thank God you are here reading this, because now is your opportunity to see very clearly how these stories have been running (and ruining) your relationships!

So it is time to change all the bullshit stories!

In this step, you are simply going to identify what some of those stories and beliefs are that have made up the identity that you have created to keep yourself safe. We have thousands of stories, so I don't expect you to identify all of them, and some of them are deep within your subconscious and will surface when you get triggered, and as you work through deeper layers of healing yourself over time.

#LOVEPRACTICE: IDENTIFY YOUR STORIES

Reflect back to your relationship patterns and I want you to identify the stories that you have been telling yourself that have led to these patterns and behaviours.

Be sure to also look at where you may have taken on other people's beliefs as your own.

One of the stories I used to hear my mum say was 'all men are bastards, some are just lesser bastards than others' - that was a big one for me to shift!

What stories have you been telling yourself about people that you have been playing out over and over?

For example: men aren't safe, men are assholes and liars, women are bitches, people always leave me.

_____
_____
_____
_____
_____
_____
_____
_____

What have you been making this mean about you?

For example: I always get rejected, I am worthless, I have to be or do XYZ to be loved, I am never enough.

_____
_____
_____
_____
_____
_____
_____
_____

What have you been making this mean about love and relationships? *For example: love hurts, love ends in abuse, relationships are too hard, I can't have a relationship and a career. It's not safe to fall in love, relationships are for everyone else, but not for me.*

_____
_____
_____
_____
_____
_____
_____
_____
_____
_____

#LOVERITUAL: RISE UP AND RECLAIM YOUR POWER

This is one of the most powerful rituals I teach and when I first shared this online it went viral with people all over the world also practicing it and posting there own version of it on Facebook!

The best time to practice this ritual is on the full moon; however, it can be done anytime and I highly recommend to repeat it, especially when you find yourself giving your power away in the future. Yes, you are still human and you will still give your power away from time to time!

1) Write out all the ways you have given your power away

Using the answers that you wrote in the above four steps write down the names of all the people, experiences, situations, and ways that you have in the past or present given your power away. You can be as specific or as general as you like. Write these down on a piece of paper.

2) Read them out and burn the paper

Read out each one and say "I rise up and I reclaim my power from..." and then follow on with each experience of giving your power away. After you have read each one out, then you burn the piece of paper and say 'SO IT IS'.

I RISE UP AND I RECLAIM MY POWER

I rise up and reclaim my power from all the men who abused me.

I rise up and reclaim my power from all the times I allowed and enabled men's abusive behaviour.

I rise up and reclaim my power from all the times I people pleased, overgave, rescued, was overly responsible and completely abandoned myself.

I rise up and reclaim my power from all the times my boundaries were crossed and all the times I allowed it.

I rise up and reclaim my power from all the times I have allowed other people's opinions of me effect my self-worth.

I rise up and reclaim my power from shame and anywhere I have been made wrong, bad and not good enough, especially towards myself.

I rise up and reclaim my power from the times I used a form of unhealthy power and control to get what I wanted and to feel safe.

I rise up and reclaim my power from all the men who have not honoured, valued, loved, and respected me, especially when I was not doing this for myself.

Reclaim Your Power in Love

I rise up and reclaim my power from the stories and beliefs that have disempowered me.

I rise up and reclaim my power from all the times I made myself small and haven't spoken up and stood in my truth.

AND SO IT IS.

Chapter 19

Coming Home to Your Inner Soulmate

"You are here to unlearn that love is conditional and remember your truth—that you are love"

Once you have fully reclaimed your power from the disempowering behaviours and stories that have been completely running your life and relationships, it's now time to turn these around and learn how to embody and show up as your completely lovable, worthy soulmate-self!

You will then complete and celebrate all of this with your very own self-marriage ceremony, or self-love commitment ceremony, if you prefer.

STEP 5: Discovering Your Empowered Truth

Wouldn't it be just amazing to be out there having relationships that prove that you are lovable, that you are worthy, that people are trustworthy, knowing that people can love, honour, and accept you just the way you are?

Now that you have discovered the stories that don't serve you, it's time to create ones that empower you, ones that are actually your soul's truth as a being who is completely made of love!

Making the Unconscious Conscious

So often I used to hear "you just have to change what you believe," which led me to plastering up affirmations all over my mirror and bedroom walls, which never, ever seemed to work, even if I said them 100 times a day!

Shifting and creating new beliefs sounds great in theory, but the problem I have seen here is that most people are trying to change their beliefs from the conscious mind, but it is our subconscious beliefs that are the ones that have to change because they are the ones that run your life. The subconscious mind is a million times more powerful than the conscious mind!

As a coach I can see people's blindspots and I ask them questions that dig into their subconscious mind which makes the unconscious become conscious. When a disempowering story surfaces and is fully seen, this is when we have the power to change it.

There are many powerful subconscious reprogramming and emotional clearing modalities out there such as EFT—Emotional Freedom Technique (Tapping), The Spiral Clearing Process, and NLP—Neural Linguistic Programming. Find the one that aligns for you, I tend to use a mix of modalities for myself and my clients.

The Power of Inner Child Healing

Without a doubt one of the most powerful practices to shift my stories is doing deep inner child work, particularly when I have taken myself back to the times I had experienced a deep wounding and created a disempowering story. I showed up for myself as the adult and I told myself what's really true about what happened.

When I took myself back to the time I got 97% on that test, I visualised myself speaking to my 7 year old self. I took little EJ's hands and looked into her eyes and I said to her "your Mum was so proud of you,

you did get everything right, the truth is that it was the teacher who did not give you the 100% marks that you actually deserved. You are enough and you are always doing enough. I am so very proud of you."

#LOVEPRACTICE: INNER CHILD TRUTH TALK

1. Visualise your younger self, either in that memory or the age you would have been when you feel you first created the disempowering story or were first wounded.
2. Take their hands and lovingly look into their eyes.
3. You are going to tell them what really happened, the real truth that you now know. Give yourself words of wisdom, speak as though you are a nurturing mother speaking to her own child. You can also tell them that you are here for them, that you will never leave them and that you love them.

If you had a parental figure leave or experienced abuse and you don't know how to explain the truth of that you can say something to your inner child like:

"I'm sorry that your parent was not able to show up for you in the way that you needed. The truth is that they were doing the best that they could whilst functioning from their own wounds and pain.

How you were treated has nothing to do with how worthy you are of love. It was only that they were incapable of loving you the way you needed and wanted to be loved. The truth is that you are so lovable and you are worthy and you are a blessing and a miracle in my life. Thank you for being here."

Download the MP3 version of this practice that guides you through the visualisation at www.ejlove.com/truthtalkmp3.

> **#LOVEBOMB: LOVING WORDS FOR YOUR INNER CHILD**
>
> The brain can't actually tell the difference between your words or someone else's.
>
> When you are wanting to hear certain words from someone, especially if they have triggered you, ask yourself "what words am I longing to hear from that person?"
>
> Then look into a mirror and say those words to yourself, similar to what you did in the earlier self-soothing inner child practice.

#LOVEPRACTICE: YOUR EMPOWERED TRUTH

Answer the questions below to discover the new stories that will create your empowered truth.

What would you like to believe to be true about men, women, and people?

For example: men are safe, trustworthy, and loving, people want the best for me, women support me fully.

_____
_____
_____
_____
_____
_____
_____
_____
_____

Coming Home to Your Inner Soulmate

What would you like to believe to be true about yourself?

For example: I am worthy, I am lovable, I am enough.

_____
_____
_____
_____
_____
_____
_____
_____
_____

What would you like to believe to be true about love and relationships?

For example: love is for me, I have relationships that are healthy and support me to grow, I can have a loving relationship and a successful career.

_____
_____
_____
_____
_____
_____
_____
_____
_____

STEP 6: Showing Up in Your Soul-Aligned Truth

Have you had the experience when you think you have changed a belief and then the same shit keeps happening and you think to yourself *"how much freaking work do I have to do to change this?"*

One of the reasons for this is because you must take ALIGNED action to help integrate your new empowered truth and make it your new reality! You have to show up inside of it to keep proving these new empowering beliefs to be true.

You may have been so used to living the old way for so long and trained other people how to treat you, but since you are now shifting out of that it means also retraining people!

This is where boundaries come in. You may also lose some friendships along the way, but you will make room for ones that honour your soul-aligned truth. What I mean by soul-aligned is that the old behaviours are no longer in alignment with who you are beyond your old conditioning. Those people who related to you in that way may no longer be able to connect with you. This may even cause some conflict, as they will not be getting their needs met from you in the way they used to as you now set boundaries around the behaviour you allow in yourself and others. This may feel like a loss at first, but eventually it will be your gain as you make space for more relationships that are aligned with your soul - who you really are! These are your soul family and soul mates that will come in various different relationship dynamics. The more you align with your inner soulmate, the more you attract this kind of soul mate energy!

Affirmations Only Work if You Align Your Behaviour

It is like saying "I love myself" and then having a cigarette, and then making yourself wrong or guilty for your choice to do that. If you are not acting how a self-loving person would then your actions are telling yourself that the affirmation you are saying actually isn't true.

If your new belief was "I am enough," the way that you would need to show up to prove this to be true would be to stop doing the things you do when you are trying to prove your worth to someone.

You lovingly call yourself on it when you are overcommitting and being overly responsible, you would stop overgiving or people pleasing to prove your value, you would notice when you are judging yourself for not being enough, and you would turn that around into compassion, appreciation, and acknowledgement of how enough you already are with words of kindness and love for yourself.

If the belief was "relationships are healthy," one of the aligned actions you will need to do is to establish healthy boundaries and learn how to consciously communicate these. You reclaim saying 'No' more often! You could also commit to practising the trigger healing practice tool in this book, amongst all the other practices in here that are helping you to have healthy relationships.

Integrating your Empowered Truth

Ultimately you have to actualise your empowered truth in your physical reality. You have to relate to yourself and other people inside of your empowered truth and this may mean you need to learn new skills to be able to do this.

Over the course of this book I have given you many tools that you can use again and again to help you integrate a soul-aligned way of being in the world. However, there is plenty more to learn and cultivate to keep aligning to who you truly are! I offer more advanced soul alignment in my Become the One program which you can find details of in the back of this book.

In the meantime, look at each of the empowering beliefs you created and ask yourself: *is there anything I need to learn and cultivate here to help me embody this and integrate it into my life?* It might be going to a course on conscious communication or learning how to set boundaries. This is why I offer further courses and workshops to dive deeper into learning conscious relationship skills. I wanted to create spaces so my readers could continue to grow and learn the skills they need to truly become who they are at the core of their soul and be able to have healthy, loving relationships from that place, whilst getting much needed support and accountability to do that!

So go ahead and get writing to the answers below—this is the part where you create aligned actions that completely change how you will show up in your relationships from now on.

These are VERY transformational times, trust me!

Another way to do is this by re-looking at the ways you gave your power away and the flipping it by asking: *if I was fully in my power how would I show up?*

#LOVEPRACTICE: SOUL-ALIGNED WAYS OF SHOWING UP

How do you need to show up and what actions do you need to take to keep proving these empowering truths to be true?

_____
_____
_____
_____
_____
_____
_____
_____
_____
_____

Coming Home to Your Inner Soulmate

What are the boundaries that you now need to set with yourself and with others?

_____
_____
_____
_____
_____
_____
_____
_____
_____
_____
_____

What are the skills that you need to learn and develop to help you live inside your empowered truth?

_____
_____
_____
_____
_____
_____
_____
_____
_____
_____
_____
_____

STEP 7: Making a Commitment to Yourself

The final piece in this process is to make a commitment to yourself to show up and honour, respect, value, and love yourself through these new actions. If you don't do it for you then how can you expect anyone else to?

This is where you now integrate everything you have processed and healed over the course of this book.

Use your answers to the questions from the previous chapters to answer these questions below and use "I commit to …"

What are the commitments that you need to make to other people?

For example: I commit to having the hard conversations rather than avoiding them.

I make a commitment to appreciate men, to love men, to see the beauty in men, to not blame them or make them wrong, but to keep learning about them and how I can have better relationships with them.

I make a commitment to listen to others' wants and needs and find ways and make agreements where we can both get our needs met.

I make a commitment to…

_____
_____
_____
_____
_____
_____
_____
_____

Coming Home to Your Inner Soulmate

What commitments are you now making to yourself?

For example: I make a commitment to know and honour my boundaries and communicate them with others.

I make a commitment to follow my intuition and practise regularly connecting to it.

I commit to holding space for myself and my emotions and to use my triggers as an opportunity for healing.

I commit to being kind to myself, to have self-empathy, self-compassion, and self-forgiveness and to love whatever arises.

I make a commitment to not overgive and to allow myself to receive more and to know that I am so damn worthy of it!

I make a commitment to...

_____
_____
_____
_____
_____
_____
_____
_____
_____
_____
_____
_____
_____

In the final chapter you will be using these commitments in the most honouring ceremony you will ever do for yourself.

#LOVERITUAL: ENERGETICALLY COMPLETE A RELATIONSHIP

The final piece to completing your healing journey is to energetically end the relationship, to cut off any ties or soul contracts that you have with this person, so you can fully move on.

A beautiful way to consciously complete a relationship is by writing a letter to the person where you own and express what you have learned from the relationship, the gifts you have received and discovered, and what you are committed to now moving forward from it.

You don't have to send the letter or read it to them, especially if it's not safe to do so. You do this as a ritual by calling in their soul and visualising them in front of you as you read it out to them. Another option is to do it with the person, but only if is safe to do so and they have agreed to do it as a way to consciously complete the relationship together.

I recommend you do this ritual with anyone you have experienced trauma or had a falling out with and still feel some incomplete energy on. You may choose to do it as a way to shift a relationship into a different way of relating to each other too, such as moving a romance into a friendship.

It is also quite useful when you have any kind of conflict with someone to take these questions, write out the answers, and then have a conversation with the person.

The following questions will guide you into the letter writing process.

- Is there anything that has been left unsaid that I really want to say?
- What am I now taking responsibility for in how I showed up in this relationship?
- What is the impact my behaviour had on them?
- What is the impact that their behaviour had on me?

Coming Home to Your Inner Soulmate

- What can I now acknowledge and appreciate the person for?
- What is my intention for this relationship now?
- What are the agreements I need to make with this person (if any)?
- What are the boundaries I need to set with this person?
- What am I now committed to with this person and/or in my other / future relationships?

At the bottom of the piece of paper write:

"I now release and revoke all the promises, agreements, commitments, and contracts I made to you in this lifetimes and all other lifetimes"

"I now release you from and revoke all the promises, agreements, commitments, and contracts you made to me in this lifetimes and all other lifetimes"

When you do this as a soul-to-soul visualisation, say these words out loud as you see them sitting in front of you and see any energy cords between you melt away.

You also have the choice to send the letter or you can burn it after you have done the ritual. But really get clear on what the purpose would be behind sending it and if this is in the highest good for your soul. When you burn the letter do this with the intention of releasing all the energy from that relationship that no longer serves you.

Chapter 20
Self-Marriage Ceremony

"You are the one you have been waiting for"

Congratulations!

You have now officially become "the one."

Your one!

The truth though is that you never had to become anything. Because you have actually been the one all along.

You just had to unlearn everything that told you that you were not!

And now you just get to BE the one.

So the day has finally come, it's time for you to walk down that aisle and say "I do" to … *yourself!*

You might not necessarily want to call this a self-marriage ceremony; you may choose to see it as a self-love commitment ceremony instead.

Why I Married Myself

On Valentine's Day 2017, I infamously said "I do" as I stood on the beach on the Gold Coast committing to love and honour myself.

Little did I know back then that my self-marriage would end up all over the internet and go viral with millions of views!

I could never have imagined that self-marriage / "sologamy" would become so big and that it would be something I would end up teaching and facilitating around the world!

The idea of marrying myself only came into my own awareness whilst I was holidaying in Bali deciding on what sort of ritual I wanted to do to complete 2016.

As it was the year of completion I was reminiscing on my time since I left my last abusive relationship and how far I had come. Oh boy, had I done some profound and deep healing work on myself as you too will have done over the course of this book!

When I finally left that relationship I made a commitment to myself that I would never, ever go through that again. I made a stand for myself and what I am worthy of in love. I told myself I would never tolerate or enable this behaviour again. But I didn't want to close my heart because of it either. I didn't want to end up a lonely angry old lady with a closed heart. I wanted to learn how to have happy, healthy love, something that had been so foreign for me in my romantic relationships.

So I refused to numb my pain like I had for ten years since the first heartbreak.

And I HEALED. I healed like I had never healed before.

I soon re-awakened to love. My own love, inside of me.

And after feeling all of this there was a moment when my heart completely broke open.

It was the moment between feeling the pain and rebuilding my relationship with myself when I felt this immense gratitude.

Self-Marriage Ceremony

I got it. I truly got it all. Why I had gone through all of this. Why it happened to me.

I then completely rebuilt my life.

Healthy boundaries were established.

Beliefs were transformed.

Patterns were rewired.

Conscious communication skills were put into practice.

Radical self-love started to become embodied.

I looked at all the ways that people hadn't honoured and committed to me and I had learned how to do this for myself first because I knew they were simply a reflection of the unhealthy relationship I had with myself.

I had to get to know myself in a whole new way. I had to build a healthy loving relationship with me and treat myself like I wanted a romantic partner to treat me.

So I spent quality time with myself.

I dated myself. Romanced myself.

Went on adventures and travelled with myself.

Got intimate with myself. Pleasured myself.

Became loyal to myself and my needs.

I also had to get really honest with myself and call myself on my own bullshit at times!

There were some hard and vulnerable conversations I had to have with myself, whilst being compassionate and reminding myself that I am still human.

At the end of the day I have to be there 100% for myself, support myself and love myself unconditionally, especially learning to love those things that I liked the least.

And this is a constant evolving and growing relationship - full of imperfections, flaws and fuck ups.

I certainly don't get 'loving myself' perfect all the time, but what I am committed to is giving this relationship a real good shot!

Because I am the only person I have to be with for the rest of my life and I am committed to making this relationship a happy, loving, healthy one!

I finally met my true soulmate the one that I had been searching for my whole life - ME!

I found myself - I found my inner soulmate.

And that is why I am able to be here now… sharing all of this with you.

To have been able to take you on this same journey to find your own inner soulmate.

When people ask me why I married myself, I often say:

"Well, why wouldn't I honour the relationship with myself, just as much, if not more than I would with another person?

When I reflected on this new way of being in relationship with myself I wanted to celebrate it and I couldn't have thought of anything more fitting than to marry myself."

Becoming a Self-Marriage Celebrant

I didn't actually end up marrying myself at the end of 2016 though, I guess you could say that's when I got engaged before I would walk down that infamous beach aisle in on the following Valentine's Day!

Self-Marriage Ceremony

I did however, facilitate my first ever self-marriage ceremony for one of my clients at the end of 2016 instead. Regan Hillyer, a successful entrepreneur, was the first woman I ever married to herself on the edge of a beautiful clifftop in Bali.

I'll never forget the feeling we both had that night that this was not only a ceremony for her, but that we were unintentionally setting the foundations of something much bigger than either of us. I said to her that I just knew that this was going to ripple effect out to other's who needed this work too. At that stage I had no plans to do any other ceremonies, let alone the hundreds of other people I have facilitated ceremonies for internationally since then!

On the same day I married myself that next year, I also married my friend and entrepreneur Linda Doktar to herself in our double self-wedding ceremony (which also went viral!). A month later I ran a woman's relationship healing retreat which completed with a group self-marriage ceremony. I have continued to facilitate this in every retreat as the power of this ceremony never ceases to amaze me - there are tears, joy and powerful shifts happening in that once-in-a-lifetime moment of self-love that words just can't give justice to. It always feels like such an incredible honour for me to be someone's self-marriage celebrant and to witness them choosing to themselves first, especially after years of giving their power away.

Eventually this led to bigger ceremonies and I soon found myself having the honour of facilitating them at large events, conferences and festivals with groups of over 100 people marrying themselves from all walks of life - men, women, single, in relationships, polyamorous - pretty much every sexuality and relationship status you can think of! I have had married couples marry themselves in double and group ceremonies and I even had a couple who had just divorced and used this as a way to consciously complete their relationship.

I have had people who have already married themselves simply come to renew their vows. I renew my own vows every year on my wedding anniversary…what a way to celebrate Valentine's Day!

So there are all kinds of reasons people choose to marry themselves, it's your own personal choice as to what your reason and intention is for your own marriage - it's all about you of course!

Self-Marriage has become a movement, one that started well before I married myself. Even though it feels to me like I just kind of fell into it, looking back now I can see that I was meant to become an integral part of being a leader of the movement particularly in Australia.

Misconceptions about Self-Marriage

There have been a lot of misconceptions in the media about what self-marriage is about and why someone would do something "so crazy" and it can often be fueled with a lot of judgement due to the misunderstanding of it. People have even called it narcissistic, but as you know a narcissist needs other people to get their supply and therefore going solo would would not give them the fuel they need to keep functioning!

When people ask me about how I have handled some of the hater's comments, I often cheekily say "well, it's good thing I married myself, because now I love myself enough to not let their judgements upset me!". I also understand that it's just their point of view based on their own experience of life and it's not personal to me.

There is a big difference between self-love and narcissism, this quote by Zero Dean says:

"Self-Love V Narcissism: Self-Love: Being content with the work-in-progress that you are. Not seeking the approval of others. Being yourself. Comparing yourself only to who you were in the past and not to others. Not thinking you are better than others.

Narcissism: None of the above"

Self-Marriage Ceremony

If you read this and can say that you are 100% good with the 'self-love' part, then I applaud you, because you must have unravelled a shitload of conditioning to be there. The reality is that most of us still seek approval from others to a degree, we compare ourselves to others and we are still learning to be who we are. It is all part of the human condition - so let's just love ourselves in the work-in-progress that we are right here - right now in this moment.

On the www.selfmarriageceremonies.com website they state that:

"Self-Marriage is a commitment to valuing and prioritizing self-love and self-care within a culture that has neglected it, left it behind, commercialized and dehumanized it. Self-Marriage is a commitment to being there for yourself, to choosing the livelihood and lifestyle that will help you grow and blossom into the most alive, beautiful, and deeply happy person you can be. Self-Marriage is a way to formalize, proclaim, share, and sanctify self-love."

A Commitment to Self-Love

And really, that's just what it is, a commitment to self-love. In a society that has made the concept of self-love-*selfish*, this is an opportunity to celebrate the importance of meeting your own needs first and practising daily self-care. It is about knowing and integrating that you don't need anyone to complete you, because you are already whole.

It is from place that you can be in a healthy relationship that deeply honours you, without relying on the other person's love and approval to validate your worthiness to be loved.

Some may say that you don't need a ceremony to do this, and I agree with that. But there is just something so special and powerful about ceremony and rituals. There is a kind of magic that happens that I can never quite explain in words.

Many of the people that I have taken through this ceremony say they feel quite differently afterwards. I have had people say to me that something in them just shifts, that they feel a new level of self-worth, that they feel the inner union between their masculine and feminine, that they experience wholeness and integration, a deeper connection to their inner being, that they feel their inner soulmate for the first time!

I also saw my self-marriage as a way of marrying my inner masculine and feminine together, a way to create sacred inner union with myself, with all these different parts of me. You may wish to see yours the same way, and as you write your vows you may want to write as though one is speaking to the other and vice versa.

My wish for you is that if you choose to do this ceremony to do it in a way that really honours yourself and the truly incredible person you are!

Attracting a Romantic Partner after Self-Marriage

Even though the purpose of the ceremony is not to attract a partner, many of the women who have done this have met a romantic partner not long afterwards. Some of my clients have gone on to teach with their partners and supported others in their self-love and relationship healing journeys and others have even facilitated their own self-marriage ceremonies. This is the true ripple effect!

I don't really teach 'soulmate manifestation' much, because I believe in 'soulmate alignment' where you align with your inner soulmate and you align with outer soulmates that will show up in various forms. In terms of a romantic soulmate there has to be a willingness to surrender to divine timing, trusting that your most soul-aligned partner will show up when they are meant to, whilst also keeping yourself energetically open and still putting in effort to go out and connect with new people, date and have fun!

Sometimes we take this 'healing' business way too seriously, so please make time for the fun things that really light you up and make you smile and laugh, even when it's not 'conscious'!

Self-Marriage Helps to Improve a Current Relationship

There are also many people who have done this ceremony who are in partnerships or already married. Doing this work on themselves and celebrating through ceremony has enhanced the relationship and connection with their partner. They learn how to commit to themselves first and communicate from that place with their partner. This is where they have been able to evolve from 'woundmate relationship' to 'soulmate relationship'. Some women even said that it completely saved their relationship!

Whatever your relationship status is, just know that it's time for you to come home to your inner soulmate.

It's time for you to look into that mirror and speak the words of love and commitment, knowing that no matter where life takes you, you will always have your own back.

That no matter whether other people love you or not, you are there to give yourself the loving attention that the little child inside of you has been longing for all along.

In the following pages of this chapter is your ceremonial guide and you can use it as you choose. You are welcome to make your ceremony completely your own as you celebrate the amazing being that you are!

#LOVECEREMONY: CEREMONY TYPE AND WEDDING LOCATION

The first decision you need to make is what kind of ceremony you would like to have.

Do you want a simple ceremony where it is just yourself?

Do you want to lush it up a bit and have a few friends to witness you?

Or do you want a huge, lavish ceremony with a whole heap of guests and a big cake, like the Italian woman did in 2017?

Or like my friend from Iceland did with an actual Priest in a real Church?!

The next question is where do you want to have it? It could be anything from the lounge room in your house, your backyard, or on top of a lush, grassy hill, in a dreamy forest or on the beach like I did.

Do you want to then have a reception afterwards? Take yourself out for a celebratory dinner and drink? Or head out and dance up a storm?!

How about a Honeymoon? You could take yourself away for a night or a week, and make love to yourself to consumate your marriage of course!

Ask yourself: *What would the soul-aligned fully self-loving version of me choose for my commitment ceremony? Write down your ideas here*

_____
_____
_____
_____
_____
_____
_____
_____
_____
_____

Self-Marriage Ceremony

THE WEDDING PLANNING LIST

All of this is optional of course, except I highly recommend definitely using the mirror, as this is the most powerful part!

- A mirror—*to fully see your inner soulmate.*

- A celebrant—*you don't really need anyone else to marry you, but you could ask a friend to guide the ceremony and hold the mirror for you as you speak into it; effectively they are acting as your celebrant. It's always fun when I get to say "I now pronounce you married to yourself!"*

- Poem—*if you choose to have a friend as a celebrant, there is a beautiful poem they can read out which is called "If you want to change the world, love yourself" by Jacqui Lalita. You will find this via google and it's on the huffpost.com website. You could also pick another poem or write your own.*

- A wedding dress or outfit—*I've had people wear everything from wedding dresses to costumes to casual clothes to even being naked! This is about you, so go with whatever honours who you are the most.*

- Flowers— *to hold or to walk down the aisle with.*

- A piece of jewellery or other accessory—*choose something that you will see on a daily basis that will remind you of the commitments you made to yourself.*

- Music—*what music or song would you like to walk down the aisle to? I also recommend to have a celebratory song that you can play at the end! I like to play "You've Got the Love" by Florence and the Machine. Choose music that whenever you hear it, it will remind you of this day.*

- An aisle to walk down—*I simply bought some fabric to make an aisle, but you don't need to have one and you can just stand in front of the mirror.*

- Rose petals—*if you have guests, have them throw these over you as you walk back down the aisle once you have said your vows.*
- A wedding cake—*yum, any excuse for cake!*
- Guests and witnesses—*who do you want to invite to your ceremony, if anyone?*
- Photos—*if you want photos to look back on your big day, ask one of your witnesses to take some photos for you. You could always go all out and hire a professional too!*

MY WEDDING PLAN LIST

Write out all the things you need to organise for your ceremony

Self-Marriage Ceremony

WRITING YOUR VOWS

This is the most important part! There are two ways I recommend to write your vows: you can either write them out following the guidance below or you can just show up at the ceremony and trust whatever wants to come out in that moment.

What I do with my clients is request that they write out all the qualities and characteristics they love about themselves and then I ask them to look at themselves through the eyes of someone who loves them.

What would that person say about you? Write all of these where there is a section to write your vows. From there you condense them down if you wish to.

Then you are to write out your commitments. You wrote these out in the previous chapter, so go back to that chapter and choose the most important commitments to yourself, you may also add more commitments.

I want you to really think about what you would be saying to someone you were marrying. If you were spending the rest of your life with someone what would you say to them?

Marrying your Inner Masculine and Feminine

I also saw my own self-marriage as a way of marrying my inner masculine and feminine together, a way to create sacred inner union with myself, with all these different parts of me coming together. You may wish to see yours the same way, and as you write your vows you could write them as though one is speaking to the other and vice versa, you may even have two sets of vows - one to the masculine and one to the feminine - it really is completely up to you as to how you want this to be!

So have a tune in now and see what comes…

My Vows

I love ... *what you love about yourself*

Self-Marriage Ceremony

I commit to … *the vows and commitments you are making to yourself*

THE SELF-MARRIAGE CEREMONY

Here comes the bride (or groom) … all dressed in … or maybe not dressed at all!

The wedding location is all set up and ready to go and it's now time to walk down the aisle and commit to yourself!

Play the music and start walking down that aisle.

When you are standing in front of the mirror look into your left eye and speak your vows.

Allow yourself to feel any emotions that may surface. You may experience everything from tears to joy to laughter.

Once you have read your vows out, if you have a piece of jewellery or accessory place this on yourself now or have someone else do it for you.

You can now be pronounced married to yourself and even cheekily kiss your hand or the mirror!

Play your celebratory song, throw the bouquet of flowers to your guests, and walk or dance back down that aisle!

Celebrate with cake, celebrate with dancing!

Celebrate everything that is you!

Celebrate that you are an absolute divine miracle!

Celebrate that you, you are the embodiment of love!

BECAUSE YOU ARE THE ONE

Conclusion

"In the end all that matters is that you gave loving your 'perfectly imperfect self' a real good shot!"

Congratulations. You did it!

You have now become "the one"—your one forever!

But the journey doesn't stop here, because this book was designed in way for you to be able to these tools and practices for the rest of your life to keep evolving, to keep growing, to keep gently loving yourself and expanding your consciousness.

Having a healthy, loving relationship with yourself isn't a one-time thing, it's a lifelong journey. So please make sure you keep this book handy so you can refer to the practices whenever you need to!

The more you deepen into these practices, the more it will become a natural habit to be conscious about your behaviour, take soul-aligned action and in turn, keep opening your heart to truly feel the love that you are.

I honestly believe that embodying all of this is the key to living a soul-connected, conscious, self-loving, happy life!

And who wouldn't want that?

Where to From Here?

Often when I learn something new, I realise how much I still have to learn!

You may have found this too whilst reading this book and realised that you still have so many more skills to learn so that you can keep showing up inside of your commitments and integrating this new way of being.

I don't believe people need to go to a whole heap of healing workshops to "fix" themselves. You aren't broken, you are just on a journey of remembering the love you are. So I love to support people to find and continue to align with their inner soulmate and keep them accountable to take actions that keep them living inside of their most empowered truth. I want everyone to be able to have happy, healthy love and that comes from embodying that love.

If you want to learn more from me, then please check out the pages at the back of the book to see how you can get continued support from either my one-on-one mentoring, workshops and retreats.

Other than that, I just wanted to truly acknowledge you for making it this far and reading this whole book! Thank you so much for trusting in me and my wisdom.

I want to also thank your inner masculine, for without him you would have not had the drive, commitment, focus, and presence to make it this far.

And acknowledging your beautiful inner feminine, for her vulnerability and openness. May she continue to awaken, open, and radiate her love out into the world.

Welcome home.

Meet EJ Love

Emmajane Love (EJ) is a Love, Relationship and Intimacy Coach as well as being practised in Tantra and Sacred Sexuality.

After years of being stuck in toxic co-dependent and narcissistic relationships, she made a vow to herself to never experience this again and that's when her journey to becoming the one truly began.

In 2017 she infamously married herself in a ceremony that turned viral on social media with millions of views. That same year she began facilitating self-marriage ceremonies for her clients and has since married hundreds of people from all over the world to themselves! She became the leader of the Self-Marriage and Sologamy movement in Australia and was recognised for this with ongoing TV and radio interviews and media articles all over the world! But her true mission behind all of this is to help stop the cycle of abuse, that at the core stems from a lack of self-love.

As EJ isn't shy about sharing her full story, she also came out on *The Morning Show Australia* proudly sharing having worked as an escort after leaving the corporate world, and then sharing how she transitioned into sexual healing work. Many of EJ's clients and followers work or have worked in the sex industry and have made this same transition with her support.

EJ has experienced the deep power of tantric practices and sexual healing where she helps people to heal and empower themselves in love, relationships, intimacy, and sex. She has created online programs, one-on-one coaching, workshops, and retreats which have helped hundreds of women and men to release shame and heal their wounds so that they can go forward in love from an empowered place and with an open heart.

Speaking from her own incredible story and experiences, she has been travelling the world since 2013, sharing her message through speaking events, podcasts, radio shows, and writing for magazines, books, and blogs.

She is most loved for her bold sharing, her openness, vulnerability, her compassion, and her somewhat controversial stories!

DEEPENING YOUR HEALING JOURNEY

Thank you for taking yourself through this healing journey, it would be such an honour if you desire to keep working together.

Become the One: Join the Program

The Become the One Online Program is highly recommended to take you deeper into this journey where you will receive video and audio trainings, powerful rituals and practices, interviews with other love and relationship experts as well as access to the private Facebook group with all the other beautiful souls who are on the same journey of self-love reclamation. You can read more at www.ejlove.com/btoprogram.

Workshops and Retreats

If you loved this book and want to dive deeper, you can find all EJ's upcoming workshops, retreats, and other programs at www.ejlove.com/events

Work with EJ One-on-One

EJ takes on a select number of clients who want to work with her privately for more personalised healing and coaching. Please go to www.ejlove.com to read about all her services and contact EJ's team via support@ejlove.com so they can set up a time for you to discuss working together.

Speaking and Media

EJ is available for media and podcast interviews as well as for speaking at events, workshops, and retreats around the world. Email media@ejlove.com to enquire about media interviews and speaking opportunities.

Bonus Sexy Gifts for You

It wouldn't truly be a complete book if I didn't give you little something to help you have an epic sex life too! Follow the links below to get access to your complimentary sexy gifts.

For Women—Deep Intimacy Masterclass
www.ejlove.com/intimacymasterclass

For Everyone—Tantric Sexual Healing Practice Audio
www.ejlove.com/tantricmp3

Reviews and Gifting this Book

If you enjoyed Become the One, would you mind taking a minute to write a review on amazon? Even a short review helps and it would mean a lot to me. If someone you know is struggling in their love life please send them a copy of this book. If you would like to order copies of this book for a company, school or group, please email support@ejlove.com.

Find Me Online

Website - *www.ejlove.com*

Sacred Sexuality Blog - *www.soulpriestess.com*

Facebook Business Page: - *www.facebook.com/ejloveofficial*

Instagram: - *www.instagram.com/ejlove_official*

Snapchat: - *www.snapchat.com/add/ejloveangel*

Twitter: - *www.twitter.com/ejloveofficial*

LinkedIN - *www.linkedin.com/in/ejlove*

Recommended Resources

EJ's Resources

Extra tools, videos, and practices that go with this book www.ejlove.com/bookresources

Spotify Playlists – www.tinyurl.com/ejsplaylists

Videos

The Power of Vulnerability TED Talk on YouTube by Brené Brown.

Soul Contracts, Twin Flames and Soulmates Redefined on YouTube by Matt Kahn

Clear Your Shit Free Video Training Series - www.clearyourshit.com

Websites

International School of Temple Arts (ISTA) - www.schooloftemplearts.org

Eliyah Tantra School - www.eliyah.com.au

The Love Coach Academy - www.lovecoachacademy.com

Emily Orum - www.heartninja.net

The Mankind Project - www.mkpau.org

Narcissism Expert - www.melanietoniaevans.com

Jeff Brown - www.soulshaping.com

Mark Rosenfeld - YouTube - www.tinyurl.com/markdatingcoach, website - www.makehimyours.com.au.

Feminine Embodiment - www.dancingeros.com

The Spiral - www.thespiral.com

Books

The Queen's Code by Alison Armstrong

Keys to the Kingdom by Alison Armstrong

The Power of Vulnerability by Brené Brown

Whatever Arises, Love That by Matt Kahn

Nonviolent Communication by Marshall Rosenberg

The Five Love Languages by Gary Chapman

Becoming the Narcissist's Nightmare by Shahida Arabi

Wired for Love by Stan Tatkin

Conscious Uncoupling by Katherine Woodward-Thomas

Communication Miracles for Couples by Jonathon Robinson

The Way of the Superior Man by David Deida

Loving What Is by Byron Katie

Letting Go: The Pathway to Surrender by David R Hawkins

Recommended Resources

The Book of Forgiving by Desmond Tutu and Mpho

Clear Your Shit by Dane Tomas

Testimonials

EJ is an amazing coach with deep knowledge and powerful techniques that truly get results. Shes compassionate, hard working and dedicated to helping women get what they deserve in life and love.

Mark Rosenfeld, Australia's No.1 Dating Coach www.makehimyours.com.au

What can I say ... EJ and the work she does has completely changed my life!

When I met EJ I was lost and disconnected from myself, I had been diagnosed with PTSD and battling severe depression.

EJ's passion and knowledge started a journey to understanding myself in a way that I had no idea even existed to me before. If you're ready to truly understand what it means to honour and love yourself then I recommend EJ and her work.

I have so much gratitude and appreciation for this woman and all the tools she has given me to live life from my heart in a way that honours myself and others. Thank you, EJ. I love you.

Moon Rose Mickie www.moonrosemickie.com

I had been working with EJ for a year, first as a relationship coach and then her workshops. Her support and love helped me through some of the toughest weeks of my life when I was struggling in my relationship.

With the tools she gave me I was able to empower myself and change toxic patterns I had been repeating my whole life. EJ has an ability to tap into what is unseen in our relationships to self and others.

Her work with awakening men has brought tears to my eyes. Her heart and compassion for what divides us as man and woman is changing the world.

Victoria Redbard, Sex Coach, www.victoriaredbard.com

I had EJ support me to commit to myself through a self-marriage ceremony and before then I had been focused on healing myself, to fix a problem and now since then, as I partnered to myself it has been about coming from a place of wholeness. Instead of looking for what is wrong, I look for what is right and this allows me to show up better and love myself intimately and deeply and stay committed. It's about remembering who I am.

David P. Wichman, Author: Every Grain of Sand, www.dpwichman.com

I pride myself on being one of the best coaches/healers out there and have looked in every direction for the kind of healer/coach that matched to what I bring to the table. And she far surpasses what I feel I bring to the table ... which is saying a lot!

She has opened up my belief to heal completely, my belief that I can step into a different dimension of power, that I can explore my sexuality in ways that not only feel extremely safe to me (given my southern Baptist upbringing and Christian beliefs), but also heal deeply abusive patterns from my past that I had done years of work on, but hadn't fully integrated what could be the results.

Testimonials

I literally could write a few pages about this woman at least so it's hard to write a teeny tiny testimonial. She is deeply intuitive. She is the perfect blend of super interesting and risqué and dangerous sexual energy that exemplifies what we think is dangerous which actually isn't dangerous … it is our deepest truth, our sexuality! She is a gem, a diamond.

And I will never stop thanking God for her. I feel that God has truly finally said "okay, Molly, here's your person that is a divine person to help you heal the deepest, darkest places of your soul …" Coming from me and my twenty-plus years of research and inner work, this says a lot.

She is an extraordinary human being, a brilliant strong healer, not too woo-woo, not too "this is what needs to happen," kind, gentle, and empowering … the perfect blend.

And she is deeply trustworthy. She is the epitome of a safe place to explore your pain, your pleasure, and most importantly … your sexual truth.

Molly Sapp, Mindset Strategist, www.mollysapp.com

EJ has made a deeply beautiful and significant contribution to the events I offer for women in the realm of sacred sexuality, relationships and intimacy. 'Enlightenment in the Bedroom' has always been extra fun when EJ Love is presenting! She is incredibly generous with sharing her expansive knowledge and insights, and highly engaging and humorous as she does so! She brings charisma and deep love to what she does and I am so grateful that she shares her gift of this imperative work.

Belinda Wearne - Creatrix of Enlightenment in the Bedroom Events and Yoni Elixir www.yonielixir.com.au

It all started when I spent a short time as a haphazard sex worker and I was watching EJ on her own sexual healing journey and then she did it: she released her free, seven-day sexual healing journey.

Everything always happening in the perfect time: I said YES and I've been forever changed since that moment.

It reawakened my sexuality and gave me a way to delve deeper and continue to expand ... and as she continues in her own lifelong apprenticeship with sexuality and relationships (as we all are doing), I've benefited.

Eventually, thanks to EJ (and Universe) providing me the opportunity I was an assistant at one of her retreats (after being a participant and client the year prior) which gave me the courage to step into my own teacher/path.

EJ is one woman who has made an impact on me. And in doing that, I know I've been able to make my own impact with many people (men and women).

Priestess Vanessa, Tantra – Kink – Shibari – Tarot @bewitchful

When I first started working with EJ, I was at a very transitional stage in my life. She helped me to find a deep sense of self-love and self-worth that I had no idea I was lacking.

During this time I was ending a 10-year relationship, leaving my career, and starting a business from scratch. Working with EJ enabled me to establish a strength within to carry this forward and really honour myself and my boundaries at a foundational level.

What led from this was an exponential transformation in my life. I would highly recommend EJ to anyone who struggles with speaking up for themselves, honouring their truth, owning their worth, or feeling the need for closure on past relationships, be it personal or professional.

Testimonials

EJ provided tools that I was able to take away and utilise in various other areas of my life. I'm truly grateful for my time working privately with EJ.

Narelle Clyde, Intuitive Visionary & Multidimensional Healer, www.narelleclyde.com

I first met EJ online, she said all I want to do is talk about sex all day and I just knew I wanted to work with her.

Since then I have done her online programmes, a couples tantra retreat and also 1:1.

My biggest breakthrough was around honouring boundaries, understanding the embodiment of the masculine and feminine, and communication between men and women.

After our 1:1 coaching I called in a soulmate relationship, it has been absolute bliss knowing how to hold space for a man whilst being able to feel safe in my vulnerability as a woman.

I could go on and on about all the ways my life has shifted since working with EJ but we'd be here for days. I can't recommend her services enough.

I love you, EJ, thank you so much for the work you do in this world x

Renelle McPherson, Author: The Melting of an Ice Maiden

I feel so blessed to have worked with EJ in various capacities of which all has been nothing short of life transformative. This woman has taught me so much about relationship with self and others, and my beautiful journey led me on a path to self-marriage.

As I began to explore deeper parts of the importance of self-love, EJ suggested a self-marriage ceremony which she facilitated for me on Valentine's Day 2017. This practice/ceremony taught me to dive even deeper within myself and become my own best friend. I am so grateful for EJ showing me a way to deepen the connection and relationship I have with myself. Her work is extremely powerful and her wisdom assists people all around the world.

Linda Liv Doktar, www.lindadoktar.com

EJ and I share the same passion for loving and encouraging men to be open, vulnerable, and connected. I follow EJ on social media and have attended her workshops before. I am astounded by her innate ability to assist men and women to open their hearts and receive the intimacy and connection our souls are crying out to receive.

Thank you, EJ, for your vulnerability, love, passion, and commitment to this work.

Jasmine Cherie, CEO of Sacred Pathways *www.jasminecherie.com.au*

How poignant that it has absolutely taken me my whole life - all my experiences and all my felts - to get to this point. I went to EJ's workshop for several reasons: to connect with and find the unknown/lost masculine within myself; to understand and honour the men of this world better.

What I received surpassed my Virgo infused, sometimes highly critical, expectations. Not only did I meet my inner stallion and embody him, he has remained with me. I've had friends comment that since working with EJ, I carry myself differently and my energy seems changed. I feel it too. My inner masculine has stepped up and taken my inner feminine as his.

Testimonials

Their union has finally found the makings of a beautiful balance within me, that I can now continue to nurture, reflect and be. I have a drive and passion that feels sustainable as I continue to work with these two energies within me. In the world exterior to me, I already loved men, however after EJ's workshop, I've come to love men even more.

I have compassion, I fully see them and am honoured by what they do for women and humanity, and for how they carry us. I embrace their polarity to the feminine. One cannot exist without the other and this workshop really brought that home for me.

I loved the spirit in which EJ Love delivered this workshop - her wisdom, ease of clarity in expressing her knowledge and her humour, allowed me to relax and be better able to meet all of me in this process. Nothing was forced, nothing was contrived.

The whole workshop was delivered with absolute humility, love and passion for what it all stood for. Her excitement for the work ignited mine more fully. I can't thank you enough EJ for all you bring to your work and to us as receivers of your gifts. I'm excited to see what more you have in store for us and to do more work with you in the future. Thank you divine Goddess - it has been an honour to partake in your offerings.

Anne O'Hoy, Body Worker/Energy Mover/Dancer/Writer

Acknowledgements

To my mum, Maureen, thank you for your compassion and understanding of my often controversial and "out there" ways. I feel incredibly blessed to have your acceptance and support, especially when it has been super vulnerable for me to share my choices with you. Thank you for sharing your wisdom and for always believing in me and loving me unconditionally through all of it. I wouldn't be the woman I am today without it.

To my dad, Max, thank you for your radical honesty and integrity, for being so proud of me, and for providing a safe space for me to share my vulnerabilities. Thank you for hearing me and providing your loving advice. Thank you for also unconditionally loving me from a deep place inside of your soul.

To my best friend Tash, thank you for always being there for me, especially when I was going through all of the abuse. Words cannot truly express how grateful I am to you, I don't know if I would be where I am today without your love, presence, and support. I will always admire your integrity and realness.

To Scott Catamas and Emily Orum, thank you for bringing your teachings to the world with such deep compassion and love and for being so generous and kind to let me share them in this book. Your generosity has helped me and so many other people that I have now gone on to teach.

To all of my friends, there are far too many of you to mention individually here, but you know who you are. Thank you for believing in me and my message and supporting me with your love and gentle encouragement which helped me to finally get this book finished! Thank you for also providing such a deep feeling of community, love, and belonging.

To all of my ex-partners and lovers mentioned in this book and others who haven't been. Thank you for all the gifts and lessons that you brought into my life. Every one of you has helped me to learn how to love myself more and for that I will be forever grateful.

To my current romantic partner, Bear, who has been such an incredible support for me as I finally birthed this book into the world. Thank you for making me feel safe enough to open my heart to you and for showing me what it's like to be with a healthy man. Thank you for helping me to experience the loving conscious relationship that I knew was possible for me. I love you.

To every single one of my clients who have entrusted in me and my wisdom and healing gifts. Thank you for being so vulnerable with me, for opening up so fully and for having the willingness to go on a deep and transformational healing journey.

Thank you to all of my past escort clients too who helped me to not only to pay for all of my personal development and business coaching that brought this book together, but you have also helped me to learn so much about men and sex.

To my inner masculine for showing up and doing the freaking work! Thank you for choosing to honour my feminine by choosing to heal instead of numb and then for holding her in her vulnerability. Without you my feminine would never have felt safe to truly shine her light out into the world as she has done!

Acknowledgements

To my inner feminine, for finally trusting in my inner masculine to hold you. Thank you for rising up and feeling the power of your vulnerability by coming out to the world even though it was scary at times. Thank you for allowing me to see that I am a beautiful woman who radiates even when I don't have all my shit together!

To "The" Dave Thompson, my bookwriting coach, who patiently waited for me for over a year to finally say "yes" to getting this book off the ground and another two years to stop procrastinating on publishing it! Thank you for providing your expertise and guidance to finally bring this magic to life. I freaking did it!!

To Nick Farley from Kimberly Photography who took the cover shot of this book! Thank you for providing so much of your time and energy in doing my photoshoots and for your fun creativity in helping me bring my most radiant self through in them.

To Erial Wheeler, my personal assistant and visibility creator. Thank you for your non-stop support helping me to bring my work into the world and doing "all the things" so that I can show up more fully in my magic. A special thank you also for the extra sprinkling of joyfulness that you bring into my world every day!

To all of my events assistants and co-facilitators thank you for believing in my message so much that you wanted to give your time to help me bring it to more people and for then shining your light and wisdom beside me.

To all of my other mentors, coaches, healers, and book authors (there have been a lot of you), thank you for showing up so fully in the world and sharing your own wisdom and your gifts so that people like me can learn from you. Thank you for helping me reclaim my power so that I have been able to go on and impact people around the world with my message.

To all my followers who watch my (sometimes controversial) videos and read (my often super long, yet interesting) Facebook posts. Thank you for reading that far and listening that long, this book would never have got this far without those of you who read and watch my videos, asked me questions, and commented on my posts. Because of your encouragement I knew this book had to be published.

And to you, my reader, thank you for choosing to love yourself enough to read this book. I hope that you continue to keep coming back home to yourself as you keep become the one that you have been waiting for.

Thank you. Thank you. Thank you.

I love and deeply appreciate you all.

Notes

Notes

Notes

Notes

Notes

Notes

Made in the USA
Monee, IL
15 September 2021